1

C000121511

Table of Contents

3

4

7

8

Gospel of Freedom

Ending Human Trafficking in Our Time

by

Dr. ant

9

11

Gospel of Freedom: Ending Human Trafficking in Our Time

Contents

17

Chapter 24: Future Directions in the Fight Against Trafficking

Innovations in Law Enforcement

Emerging Research and Education

The Role of Young Leaders and Activists

A Gospel of Freedom

Appendix A: Appendix

Resources for Further Reading

Contact Information for Organizations Fighting Human Trafficking

Glossary of Terms

Chapter 26: Acknowledgments

Introduction: The Call to End Human Trafficking

Human trafficking, a grave violation of human dignity and freedom, demands an urgent call to action. It's a modern-day form of slavery that ensnares millions across the globe, including within the borders of the United States. This introduction aims to illuminate the darkness surrounding this crucial issue, rallying a diverse audience-devout Roman Catholics, college professors, law enforcement officers, politicians, lawyers, and life advocates-to unite in a common cause. Our goal is to expose the horrors of human trafficking in America and galvanize a collective movement towards its eradication, offering effective ways for everyone to get involved and contribute to ending this scourge.

Human trafficking, in its most diabolical form, strips individuals of their inherent human rights, subjecting them to exploitation for labor, sexual servitude, or both. This nefarious crime hides in plain sight, affecting our communities, towns, and cities. It preys upon the vulnerable, exploiting weaknesses and offering a false promise of hope and employment. The complexity and clandestineness of human trafficking operations necessitate a sophisticated and multidimensional approach to combat it effectively. Our discourse seeks to inspire a sense of responsibility and action among all segments of society, guided by a profound respect for human dignity that lies at the heart of our moral and ethical compass (Bigio and Vogelstein, 2021).

The magnitude of human trafficking in America is alarming, with thousands falling victim to its clutches each year. Despite significant efforts to combat this issue, it persists, growing more insidious as traffickers evolve their methods. This calls for relentless perseverance and innovation in our strategies, harnessing the power of collaboration across various sectors of society. Education, awareness, and vigilance can serve as powerful tools in identifying and rescuing victims, while also preventing potential trafficking situations before they occur.

The Catholic Church, among others, has long championed the cause of the oppressed and voiceless. Its teachings and traditions offer a unique perspective on human trafficking, rooted in the sanctity of human life and the imperative to love and serve one's neighbor. By integrating theological reflections with practical action, the Church can play a pivotal role in mobilizing communities and raising awareness about this issue. Its network and influence can significantly support the broader efforts to dismantle trafficking networks and provide solace and rehabilitation to victims.

Legislation, both at the federal and state levels, serves as a critical framework for addressing human trafficking. Yet, laws alone are insufficient if not rigorously enforced and complemented by policies that address the root causes of trafficking, such as poverty, inequality, and demand for trafficked labor and sexual services. Advocacy for stronger, more comprehensive laws, alongside efforts to ensure their implementation, is crucial for a robust anti-trafficking response.

The identification of trafficking victims is fraught with challenges, given the covert nature of these crimes. Victims often suffer in silence, either out of fear, coercion, or misidentification. Training for law enforcement, healthcare professionals, educators, and other frontline workers is vital for recognizing the signs of trafficking and providing a lifeline to those ensnared by it (Campbell and Zimmerman, 2017).

Organizations, both secular and faith-based, are instrumental in the fight against human trafficking. Their work in awareness-raising, victim support, and advocacy for policy change embodies the multi-faceted response required to combat trafficking. By spotlighting their efforts and encouraging public support for their initiatives, we can amplify the impact of their invaluable work.

This introduction, and the book that it prefaces, aims to serve as a beacon of hope and a call to action. Through a blend of scientific analysis, rhetorical persuasion, and biblical empathy, it seeks to engage the reader's heart and mind. The fight against human trafficking is not solely the responsibility of law enforcement or policymakers; it is a collective moral obligation that requires each of us to contribute towards a more just and compassionate society.

As we move forward, let us remember that human trafficking is not an abstract issue-it involves real people with inherent dignity. The quest to end trafficking is not just a fight against a crime, but a solemn vow to uphold the value of every human life. Together, armed with knowledge, faith, and a collective determination, we can forge a path towards freedom for all.

Let this book, and the collaborative efforts it inspires, serve as a testament to our shared humanity and enduring commitment to liberate the captive, protect the vulnerable, and heal the wounded. In doing so, we echo the call for justice that resounds in every human heart, compelling us to action in the pursuit of a world free from the shackles of human trafficking.

Understanding Human Trafficking in America

Human trafficking, a grave violation of human rights, thrives in the shadows of American society. It's an issue that mirrors the deepest abyss of moral decay, ensnaring thousands of individuals, depriving them of their freedom, and subjecting them to exploitation. At its core, human trafficking is a complex phenomenon that manipulates and capitalizes on human vulnerabilities for profit. In defining human trafficking, it's essential to recognize its multifaceted nature, encompassing forced labor, sexual exploitation, and servitude (U.S. Department of Homeland Security, 2019). This definition provides a foundation for addressing the issue, acknowledging that anyone, regardless of age, gender, or background, can become a victim under certain coercive and deceptive conditions.

The scope of human trafficking in America is vast and deeply concerning. It's a pervasive issue that spans across states, with each region facing its unique challenges and patterns of trafficking. Statistics offer a chilling glimpse into the magnitude of the problem, with thousands of trafficking cases reported annually to the National Human Trafficking Hotline. These figures, however, likely represent only a fraction of the total incidents, as many cases go unreported or undetected due to the hidden and insidious nature of trafficking activities (Polaris Project, 2020). By understanding the scope of the issue, with a particular focus on state-by-state statistics, stakeholders can tailor their interventions and strategies to address the specific needs and dynamics of their communities.

Addressing human trafficking in America demands a concerted effort from all sectors of society. Law enforcement, policymakers, educators, healthcare professionals, and the wider community all have crucial roles to play in combatting this scourge. The call to action is clear: it's not just about raising awareness but also about implementing practical, effective measures to prevent trafficking, protect victims, and prosecute perpetrators. It requires a multifaceted approach that combines stringent legislation, comprehensive support systems for survivors, and, critically, a societal commitment to eradicating the demand that fuels trafficking networks (U.S. Department of State, 2020). In this collective endeavor, every action, no matter how small, contributes to the broader fight against human trafficking, forging a path towards freedom and dignity for all.

Defining Human Trafficking

In the quest to illuminate the grave issue of human trafficking within the tapestry of American society, it is paramount to distill a clear, comprehensive definition of the term. Human trafficking, at its core, is a severe violation of human rights, characterized by the exploitation of individuals through coercion, deception, or force for the purposes of labor, sexual exploitation, or both. This multifaceted phenomenon transcends mere criminal activity, embedding itself in the very sinews of societal, economic, and cultural frameworks (Bales et al., 2005). Unlike the trade of goods, this insidious trade deals with lives, stripping victims of their dignity, autonomy, and freedom, reducing them to mere commodities in a market driven by demand and profit (U.S. Department of State, 2020). This exploitation is not confined to the shadows but proliferates in the open, its ubiquity a testament to the imperatives of vigilance, education, and action. The moral imperative to combat human trafficking is not solely the province of law enforcement or political entities but a universal call to which every segment of society must respond. The odyssey towards eradicating this scourge commences with understanding its foundations, fostering an environment where every individual is seen not as a potential commodity, but as an inviolable bearer of dignity and rights (International Labour Organization, 2017).

Forms of Human Trafficking In the endeavor to dissect the multifaceted issue of human trafficking, it is paramount to acknowledge its various manifestations. Human trafficking, a grievous blight on humanity, morphs to exploit individuals across different sectors, leading to a spectrum of abuse and exploitation. This chapter seeks to illuminate the diverse forms of trafficking that shadow our communities, beckoning a united and informed response.

At its core, human trafficking is the act of coercing, forcing, or deceiving individuals into situations of exploitation for the trafficker's gain. This exploitation can manifest in myriad ways, each with its distinct characteristics and challenges. While most discussions on human trafficking pivot around sex trafficking, labor trafficking is equally pervasive and pernicious. Labor trafficking victims are often ensnared in work environments where they are exploited for their labor, receiving little to no compensation and living in inhumane conditions.

Sex trafficking, a form that has garnered significant attention, involves the exploitation of individuals through coercion, force, or deceit into commercial sex acts. This form of trafficking preys upon the vulnerabilities of its victims, often employing psychological manipulation alongside physical control to maintain compliance (Litam, 2017).

Child trafficking, an especially heinous form, involves the exploitation of children for various purposes such as labor, begging, involvement in armed conflicts, and sex trafficking. The trafficking of children is a global issue, with various cultures and economic systems perpetuating the demand for exploited child labor and sexual exploitation (Beryer, 2004).

Forced marriage, though often overlooked, is a form of trafficking where individuals are compelled to marry against their will. This practice not only deprives individuals of their autonomy but also subjects them to a life of servitude and, in many cases, sexual exploitation and domestic violence.

Debt bondage, another prevalent form, traps individuals in a cycle of debt that becomes impossible to repay. Workers are coerced into laboring for little or no pay, with the promise of eventual freedom that perpetually remains out of reach. This form of exploitation is particularly common in sectors with significant labor demands and low regulatory oversight.

Human trafficking also extends to the forced recruitment of children and adults into armed conflicts, a practice that devastates communities and perpetuates cycles of violence and exploitation.

Organ trafficking, while less commonly discussed, represents a dark corner of human trafficking where individuals are exploited for their organs, which are sold on the black market for transplants. Victims of this form of trafficking are often deceived or coerced into surgeries to remove organs or are outright abducted and mutilated (Bowden, 2013).

The digital age has also ushered in new forms of exploitation, with traffickers leveraging technology to exploit and control victims. Cyber trafficking involves the use of digital platforms to recruit, exploit, or sell access to victims for various forms of exploitation, including sexual exploitation and forced labor.

Beyond these forms, human trafficking manifests in diverse and evolving ways, responding to and exploiting socioeconomic conditions, conflict situations, and technological advancements. The complexity of trafficking forms underscores the necessity for a multifaceted and adaptive response to effectively combat this scourge.

To battle these various forms of trafficking, it is essential to foster a comprehensive understanding among all societal sectors. Education, law enforcement, legal frameworks, and community engagement must be harmonized in a concerted effort to dismantle the structures that enable human trafficking.

The moral and ethical imperatives to combat human trafficking resonate with the core teachings of various faith traditions, which advocate for the protection and dignity of every human being.

Engaging communities of faith in the fight against trafficking can amplify efforts to raise awareness, support victims, and challenge the societal norms that allow exploitation to flourish (Lee, 2013).

Finally, the collaboration between national and global entities is crucial in addressing the international dimensions of human trafficking. Trafficking networks often transcend borders, requiring an orchestrated international response to effectively disrupt these criminal activities.

In conclusion, the battle against human trafficking demands a nuanced understanding of its various forms. By shining a light on the dark realities of exploitation and rallying together as a united front, society can strive towards eradicating this blight, restoring dignity and freedom to its countless victims. The task is formidable, but the collective resolve can pave the way towards a future where human trafficking is relegated to the annals of history.

The Scope of the Problem

The malignant growth of human trafficking in America is a contemporary scourge that mirrors the darkest facets of our society, necessitating a profound and collective introspection. This vile trade, ingeniously cloaked in the shadows of legality and everyday transactions, has ensnared countless souls, leaving a trail of despair and degradation in its wake. The magnitude of this crisis, though daunting, is not insurmountable, with studies revealing an alarming proliferation of cases across all states, painting a distressing picture of the pervasiveness of this issue. It's imperative to acknowledge that behind these cold statistics are human beings ensnared in a relentless cycle of exploitation and suffering, underscoring the urgent need for a robust, multidimensional approach aimed at eradicating this blight from our midst. A poignant analysis by (Gozdziak and Collett, 2005) sheds light on the grim reality, revealing a substantial increase in identified trafficking cases, corroborating the insidious nature and the escalating scope of this problem within American borders. Concurrently, the Polaris Project's comprehensive study (2020) delineates the multifaceted nexus of trafficking networks, further emphasizing the critical necessity for concerted efforts in dismantling these oppressive structures. As we navigate through this quagmire, let us be guided by our moral compass, fortified by empirical evidence and galvanized by our collective resolve to restore dignity and justice to the afflicted.

State-by-State Statistics As we transition from understanding the broader scope of human trafficking in America, it is crucial to zoom into a more granulated view, revealing the heartbreaking variability and prevalence of this scourge across states. Each state, with its unique legislative framework, demographics, and economic conditions, presents a different facet of the human trafficking dilemma. The statistics we are about to delve into are not just numbers but represent human beings entrapped in exploitative situations against their will.

To commence, let's consider California, often cited for its high incidence of human trafficking due to its vast economy, significant immigrant population, and status as a border state. According to the National Human Trafficking Hotline, California consistently reports the highest number of human trafficking cases in the U.S. (Tillyer et al., 2023). These cases span across sex and labor trafficking, underscoring the multifaceted nature of trafficking operations within the state.

Shifting to Texas, another border state, the narrative is similarly grim. Texas benefits from and suffers due to its extensive border with Mexico, a factor that complicates the state's trafficking dynamics. Texas' diverse industries, including agriculture and construction, are sectors commonly associated with labor trafficking. The state's urban centers, such as Houston and Dallas, are significant hubs for sex trafficking (Winterdyk et al., 2011).

Contrastingly, in smaller states like New Hampshire, the human trafficking problem might appear less pronounced but remains equally malignant. New Hampshire, due to its location, serves as a transit state for trafficking routes in the. Here, the scale might be smaller, but the impact on individual lives is profound and devastating.

Moving towards the Southeast, Florida emerges as another critical point of interest due to its tourism industry, which unfortunately provides a guise for traffickers to exploit vulnerable individuals. Florida's trafficking cases often highlight the brutal reality of sex trafficking in tourist areas, alongside significant instances of labor trafficking in agriculture (Brenner, 2006).

In the Midwest, states like Illinois exemplify the urban dimension of human trafficking. Chicago, as a major metropolitan area, draws a significant number of human trafficking victims into commercial sex operations and forced labor scenarios. These cases often involve complex networks that exploit both domestic and international victims.

The varied landscape of human trafficking across states clearly illustrates that this is not an issue confined to any single region or demographic in America. It's pervasive, reaching every corner of the nation, from rural areas to bustling cities. This geographical spread not only underscores the complexity of combating trafficking but also illustrates the adaptability of traffickers to exploit socio-economic and legislative discrepancies between states.

Moreover, the statistics point towards a concerning trend of underreporting and lack of identification. Many victims do not come forward, and many witnesses do not recognize the signs of trafficking or do not know how to help. This gap significantly hampers efforts to provide justice and support to victims, emphasizing the need for enhanced public education and stronger identification efforts by authorities.

Additionally, the statistics drive home the importance of state-level legal frameworks and resources dedicated to fighting human trafficking. While federal laws provide a baseline, the effectiveness of anti-trafficking efforts often hinges on how well states can implement, enforce, and augment these laws, tailoring interventions to their specific trafficking profiles.

Importantly, these statistics should serve not solely as a measure of the enormity of the issue but as a catalyst for action. Understanding the distinct challenges and trends within each state can help in crafting targeted strategies that address local trafficking dynamics effectively (Tillyer et al., 2023).

Furthermore, this granular look at state statistics calls for a multi-disciplinary approach in combating human trafficking. Collaboration across law enforcement, legal sectors, social services, and communities is critical to dismantle trafficking networks and support victims. Each state's unique position demands a customized blend of enforcement, prevention, and victim support services.

Lastly, the role of the community cannot be understated in identifying and stopping human trafficking. Public vigilance, supported by education and awareness campaigns, can significantly disrupt trafficking operations. Communities informed about their state's specific trafficking issues are better equipped to protect vulnerable populations and assist victims.

In conclusion, as we sift through the state-by-state statistics, let us be reminded of the urgency and responsibility we bear in eradicating human trafficking. No state is immune, and no individual is too distant to make a difference. It is through our combined efforts, informed by the realities illuminated by these statistics, that we can hope to dismantle the chains of modern-day slavery.

Chapter 2: The Catholic Perspective on Human Trafficking

The Catholic faith, rooted deeply in the sanctity of human dignity and the moral foundations of society, confronts the egregious sin of human trafficking as a grave violation against God's created order. This chapter delves into the Catholic Church's theological considerations and pastoral responses to human trafficking, underpinning the moral outrage against this crime with a rigorous theological framework (Pati, 2014). In essence, the Church's teachings position human trafficking as an affront to the inherent dignity of the human person, created in the image of God. It articulates a call to action for the faithful, leveraging the Church's extensive network to mobilize resources, provide support to survivors, and engage in advocacy to eradicate trafficking. The Holy See has consistently condemned trafficking, endorsed international efforts and urged nations to protect the vulnerable (Pontifical Council for Justice and Peace, 2004). This chapter not only examines the ecclesial documents and Papal encyclicals that articulate the Church's stance but also highlights the active engagement and initiatives led by Catholic organizations. The collective effort of the Church, from theological reflection to practical action, mirrors the call of the Gospel to "set the oppressed free" (Isaiah 58:6), igniting a beacon of hope amidst the darkness of exploitation and slavery. In doing so, the Catholic perspective enriches the broader discourse on human trafficking, providing a robust moral and ethical framework for understanding and combating this pervasive issue.

Theological Reflections

The Catholic perspective on human trafficking intricately intertwines with deep theological convictions about the inherent dignity of every human being. This belief, rooted in Scripture and Tradition, compels a call to action against the evils of human trafficking, which stands as a grave violation of this dignity. This section explores these theological foundations and reflects on how they inform the Church's response to the plight of millions ensnared in modern-day slavery.

At the heart of Catholic teaching is the imago Dei, the belief that every person is made in the image and likeness of God (Genesis 1:27). This foundational concept underpins the Church's unwavering commitment to defending human dignity. In the context of human trafficking, this means recognizing each victim as a cherished child of God, not merely a statistic or a case study. The degradation and subjugation that trafficked individuals endure are affronts not only to their dignity but also to the Creator who endowed them with it.

Scriptural mandates to protect the vulnerable and seek justice for the oppressed further fuel the Church's resolve. Passages such as Proverbs 31:8-9 exhort believers to "Speak up for those who cannot speak for themselves, for the rights of all who are destitute. Speak up and judge fairly; defend the rights of the poor and needy." In light of such teachings, apathy or inaction in the face of human trafficking can never be justified within a Catholic framework.

The Parable of the Good Samaritan (Luke 10:25-37) stands as a powerful testament to the call to mercy and neighborly love. In this narrative, Jesus illustrates that our neighbor is anyone in need, including those trapped in situations of exploitation and abuse. This parable challenges Catholics to see the face of Christ in the victims of trafficking and to extend compassion and assistance without hesitation or prejudice.

The Catholic Church also draws upon its rich sacramental and liturgical life to lament the tragedy of human trafficking and to intercede for its victims. Through Masses, prayers, and vigils dedicated to this cause, the faithful are reminded of their responsibility to combat this scourge and pray for the liberation and healing of those affected.

Social doctrine, encapsulated in papal encyclicals such as Rerum Novarum and Caritas in Veritate, provides a further layer of theological insight. These documents advocate for justice, solidarity, and the protection of workers' rights, themes deeply relevant to the fight against trafficking. Pope Francis, in particular, has been vocal about the moral imperative to confront modern slavery, emphasizing that this battle is integral to the

Gospel message of freedom and redemption (Eliasaputra et al., 2022).

The concept of the common good, another cornerstone of Catholic social teaching, impels collective action against human trafficking. It suggests a society where conditions allow individuals to reach their fulfillment more fully and easily—conditions starkly negated by human trafficking. Thus, working to eradicate trafficking is not only about aiding individual victims but about fostering a more just and humane world for all.

Moral theology, with its emphasis on conscience and moral decision-making, encourages Catholics to consider their complicity, however indirect, in the systems that perpetuate trafficking. This might involve reflecting on consumer habits, advocacy for just laws, or participation in initiatives that support ethical labor practices.

The Church's vision of eschatology, or the theology of the last things, offers hope that evil will not have the last word. In the face of the often-overwhelming magnitude of human trafficking, this hope fuels perseverance in the long and arduous struggle against it. It reassures the faithful that their efforts are sown in the fertile ground of God's promise of a redeemed creation where justice and peace will ultimately prevail.

This theological reflection on human trafficking crystallizes into a clear call to action for Catholics. It beckons them to advocate for justice, provide support to survivors, educate themselves and others, and pray fervently for an end to this heinous crime.

In addition to these spiritual and moral responses, there is a need for practical engagement. The Church's extensive network of charities, educational institutions, and advocacy groups positions it uniquely to lead and support initiatives against trafficking. From providing shelter and rehabilitation services to survivors, to lobbying for stronger laws and enforcement, Catholics are called to be at the forefront of this fight (Campbell and Zimmerman, 2014).

Ultimately, the Catholic reflection on human trafficking is a reminder that this battle is not just political, economic, or social- it is fundamentally a spiritual struggle against a profound evil. It demands a response that is commensurate with the Christian call to love God and neighbor in every circumstance, particularly where the dignity and freedom of the most vulnerable are at stake.

The fight against human trafficking, then, becomes a tangible expression of the Church's mission in the world. It is a concrete way in which Catholics live out their faith, bear witness to the values of the Gospel, and contribute to the building of the

Kingdom of God here on earth. Engaging in this struggle is not optional; it is an essential part of what it means to follow Christ in today's world (Eliasaputra et al., 2022).

In conclusion, the Catholic approach to human trafficking is rooted in a profound theological vision that compels both reflection and action. It is a call to see the face of Christ in those who suffer and to hear the Gospel as a mandate to bring freedom to captives. In a world marred by the sin of trafficking, the Church's voice and actions are vital beacons of hope, guiding efforts to restore dignity, justice, and peace to the most marginalized among us.

The Church's Teachings and Responses

Within the Judeo-Christian tradition, human dignity stands as a cornerstone, reflecting the belief that every individual is created in the image and likeness of God. This foundational principle is vehemently upheld by the Roman Catholic Church, which has long considered the fight against human trafficking not just a matter of human rights, but a profound moral imperative. It's within this context that the Church's teachings and responses to human trafficking need to be understood and appreciated.

The Church's magisterium, through various encyclicals and statements, has consistently condemned human trafficking as an egregious offense against human dignity and freedom. It categorizes human trafficking as a modern form of slavery that directly contravenes God's law. This viewpoint is deeply embedded in the Church's social doctrine, which champions the sanctity of human life and the inherent dignity of every person.

Pope Francis, in particular, has been vociferous in his condemnation of human trafficking, describing it as a "crime against humanity" and a "wound on the body of contemporary society". His papacy has seen a renewed vigor in the Church's mission to fight this scourge. Under his leadership, the Vatican has hosted several conferences aimed at raising awareness and fostering collaborative efforts among different stakeholders to combat human trafficking(Kayula, 2010).

In response to the growing menace of human trafficking, the Catholic Church has initiated numerous programs and actions worldwide. Caritas Internationalis, for instance, runs several projects offering protection, support, and rehabilitation for victims of human trafficking. These initiatives are a testament to the Church's commitment to healing and supporting those who have been subjected to this grave injustice.

Beyond individual efforts, the Church has also been instrumental in promoting policy changes and encouraging legislative action against human trafficking. By leveraging its significant global influence, the Church has advocated for stronger laws and enforcement mechanisms to deter traffickers and safeguard the rights and dignity of victims.

Theology also plays a critical role in the Church's response to human trafficking. The Church teaches that every action to counter human trafficking reflects the Gospel's mission to set the oppressed free and restore broken lives. Through its pastoral care, the Church seeks not only to provide physical release from the chains of trafficking but also spiritual healing.

This theological perspective is closely tied to the Church's social justice teachings, which call for a preferential option for the poor and vulnerable. Victims of human trafficking are among the most marginalized and exploited individuals in society, and the Church's mission to serve them is seen as a direct reflection of Jesus's own ministry.

The Church also emphasizes the importance of community awareness and education in combating human trafficking. Through its vast network of parishes and schools, the Church has undertaken programs to educate the faithful about the realities of human trafficking and inspire them to act. This grassroots approach is crucial in preventing trafficking and supporting survivors within communities (Carson, 2016).

Faith-based healing programs form another pillar of the Church's response to human trafficking. Recognizing the profound trauma experienced by victims, the Church offers spiritual and psychological support to help them rebuild their lives. Services such as counseling, spiritual direction, and sacramental ministry are provided to nurture healing and hope among survivors.

In addition to direct interventions, the Church's advocacy extends to the economic factors underpinning human trafficking. It calls for ethical consumption, fair trade, and corporate responsibility to ensure that economic practices do not inadvertently support trafficking. Through this holistic approach, the Church seeks to address both the symptoms and root causes of trafficking.

Internationally, the Church plays a pivotal role in fostering collaboration among various entities working against human trafficking. The Pontifical Academy of Social Sciences, for example, has been a platform for dialogue and cooperation between religious leaders, policymakers, and civil society organizations dedicated to eradicating trafficking.

The Church's comprehensive response to human trafficking is deeply intertwined with its broader mission of social justice and care for the marginalized. It's a mission that resonates with the prophetic call to justice we find throughout Scripture and the Church's tradition (Kayula, 2010).

Lastly, it's worth noting that the Church's engagement with the issue of human trafficking is not static but evolving. As the complexities of human trafficking evolve, so too does the Church's response, adapting to new challenges and seeking more effective ways to combat this global injustice.

In conclusion, the Catholic Church's teachings and responses to human trafficking are a profound manifestation of its commitment to human dignity, social justice, and the Gospel mandate. While the road ahead is daunting, the Church remains steadfast in its resolve to fight human trafficking through faith, action, and collaboration.

Chapter 3: Laws and Regulations

In the labyrinthine battle against human trafficking, the cornerstone of our armamentarium lies in the intricate weave of laws and regulations etched across the legislative fabric of the United States. At the heart of this battle, the Trafficking Victims Protection Act (TVPA) stands as a bastion, first enacted in 2000 and reauthorized multiple times to adapt to the evolving faces of trafficking. This act delineates the federal government's approach, encapsulating provisions for victim identification, protection, and support, while equipping law enforcement with the necessary tools to combat traffickers with rigor (Atkinson et al., 2016). Diving deeper into the stratums of governance, state-level legislations emerge with variegated hues, reflecting the unique challenges and exigencies of the local contexts. Notably, states like California and New York have been at the fore, pioneering stringent laws and comprehensive measures that aim not only to punish the perpetrators but also to shield the victims from retribution and stigma, thereby fostering a conducive environment for recovery and reintegration (Wooditch, 2012).

However, the effectiveness of these laws is contingent upon the finesse of their implementation and the vigilance of the enforcing bodies. It is this synergy between the letter of the law and the spirit of its execution that can sculpt a refuge for the victims and a fortress against the scourge of human trafficking. Thus, as we delve further into the analysis of these legal frameworks, their scope, and their impact, it becomes imperative to contemplate their alignment with the moral compass that guides our collective conscience, urging us to forge a sanctuary where dignity, freedom, and justice are not just inscribed in stone but are lived realities for all (Brown, 2010).

Current Federal Legislation

At the heart of the United States' legal framework against human trafficking lies a cornerstone piece of legislation known as the Trafficking Victims Protection Act (TVPA) of 2000 and its subsequent reauthorizations. This act represents the first comprehensive federal law to address trafficking in persons, setting forth a wide array of measures aimed at the eradication of human trafficking both domestically and internationally. Among its provisions, the TVPA establishes severe penalties for trafficking offenses, mandates restitution to victims, and outlines protections and services for survivors, thereby laying a solid legal foundation upon which further actions can be built (Berardinis, 2013).

Since its inception, the TVPA has undergone several reauthorizations, each refining and expanding its scope to adapt to the evolving nature of human trafficking. The law propels federal agencies to coordinate efforts, enhances victim assistance programs, and increases public awareness. Its legislative evolution is indicative of a growing acknowledgment within the political sphere of the necessity to combat trafficking with a multifaceted and dynamic approach. Recent amendments have focused on improving victim identification, expanding services for survivors, enhancing penalties for traffickers, and fostering international cooperation. Through these means, the legislation seeks not only to prosecute offenders but also to prevent trafficking and protect victims, embodying a holistic approach to the plight (De Angelis, 2012).

Furthermore, the reauthorizations of the TVPA reflect a bi-partisan commitment to strengthening the United States' stance against human trafficking, demonstrating the issue's unique capacity to unite individuals across the political spectrum in a common cause. It is through this legislative body that the nation articulates its dedication to ending the scourge of trafficking, asserting both moral and legal imperatives to act decisively. The legislation, thus, serves as a testament to the collective will to uphold the dignity and rights of every individual, aligning with universal ethical principles and reinforcing America's commitment to freedom and justice for all (Atkinson et al., 2016).

The Trafficking Victims Protection Act (TVPA) As we turn our focus to the vital legislative strides made in the battle against human trafficking, the Trafficking Victims Protection Act (TVPA) of 2000 marks a cornerstone in U.S. federal efforts to combat this grave injustice. At its core, the TVPA serves not only as a legal framework but also as a moral compass, guiding the nation in its quest to eradicate the exploitation of human beings for labor and sexual purposes.

The act, initially passed with broad bipartisan support, reflects a deep understanding of human trafficking as a multifaceted crime that requires a comprehensive approach. It acknowledges the nuanced needs of victims while imposing stringent penalties on perpetrators. The legislation's dual focus on victim protection and the prosecution of traffickers aligns with principles of justice and human dignity that resonate deeply within the Catholic ethos, as well as broader humanitarian values.

The TVPA's definition of trafficking is expansive, recognizing that coercion, fraud, or force are often used to exploit individuals. This crucial acknowledgment has paved the way for law enforcement and social services to identify and aid victims who might not self-identify as such due to fear, manipulation, or misinformation by their traffickers. Understanding this dynamic is crucial for all involved in the fight against trafficking, from policymakers to those providing direct support to victims (Hendrix, 2010).

One of the act's significant contributions is the establishment of the Tier system, which evaluates and ranks governments worldwide based on their efforts to combat human trafficking. This global perspective underscores the universal moral imperative to challenge injustices and protect the vulnerable, irrespective of national borders. It serves as a reminder that human trafficking is not an isolated issue but a global epidemic that demands collaborative and proactive international efforts.

Moreover, the TVPA has led to the creation of the T-Visa, providing a path to legal residency for victims of trafficking who cooperate in the prosecution of their traffickers. This aspect of the act reflects a profound commitment to restoring the dignity and rights of victims, offering them a chance for a new life free from exploitation. The message it conveys aligns with the teachings of mercy and redemption intrinsic to the Catholic faith and other religious and ethical traditions (Coonan, 2006).

The act also mandates the establishment of the Office to Monitor and Combat Trafficking in Persons, which conducts annual reports and spearheads initiatives to reduce human trafficking. This office represents an ongoing, institutionalized commitment to addressing trafficking, ensuring that efforts to combat this crime are sustained and adaptive to changing circumstances and challenges.

Despite these positive strides, the enactment of the TVPA also brings to light the complexity of combating human trafficking. Challenges such as underreporting by victims, the hidden nature of the crime, and the difficulty of prosecuting traffickers necessitate continued innovation and dedication. Engaging in this fight requires not only legal and political action but also a transformation of societal attitudes that tolerate or perpetuate exploitation (Beale, 2018).

Furthermore, the TVPA emphasizes the importance of victim services, including rehabilitation and assistance programs. This holistic approach acknowledges that rescue is just the first step in a long journey towards healing and integration for survivors. Support services aligned with this act mirror the principle of caritas, emphasizing the need for compassionate care and empowerment of those who have suffered exploitation.

As the TVPA has evolved through its reauthorizations, it has expanded provisions to address emerging challenges and to refine strategies for prevention, protection, and prosecution. This indicates a recognition that laws must grow and adapt to effectively confront the changing tactics of traffickers and the evolving needs of victims.

At its heart, the TVPA is not merely a legal instrument but a call to action for all sectors of society. It challenges individuals, communities, and institutions to not only comply with regulations but to actively engage in the cultural shift required to dismantle the systems and beliefs that enable human trafficking.

For devout Catholics, college professors, law enforcement, politicians, lawyers, life advocates, and all concerned citizens, the TVPA serves as both a guide and a challenge. It beckons us to unite in a common purpose, employing our unique gifts and positions to foster a world where all people can live free from exploitation. It is through collective, concerted action that we can transform this vision into reality, adhering to the moral imperatives that drive us to seek justice and protect the vulnerable amongst us (Hendrix, 2010).

The journey towards fully realizing the goals of the TVPA is ongoing, requiring perseverance, collaboration, and an unwavering commitment to humanity's inherent dignity. It is a path that demands not only legal and political diligence but a deep, abiding compassion that transcends differences and inspires universal solidarity.

In conclusion, the Trafficking Victims Protection Act represents a foundational step in the ongoing struggle against human trafficking. Yet, it also serves as a reminder that legislation alone cannot end this scourge. It requires the active participation of every segment of society to create an environment where human dignity is upheld, and trafficking is relegated to the annals of history. Together, drawing upon our shared values and convictions, we can move closer to a world where freedom and justice prevail for all.

State-Level Legislation

Within the complex framework designed to combat human trafficking, state-level legislation occupies a critical, albeit varied, position. Each state, acting as an individual entity within the federal system, crafts distinctive laws that address the nuances of human trafficking within its borders. This diverse legal landscape not only demonstrates the multifaceted nature of human trafficking but also the tailored approaches states adopt to mitigate it. Some states have enacted robust laws that offer comprehensive victim support services, while others focus on the punitive measures against traffickers. Yet, the effectiveness of these laws largely depends on enforcement mechanisms and the synergy between state and federal regulations.

Notably, states have pioneered innovative legislative models that have subsequently influenced national policy. For instance, safe harbor laws, which protect child victims of trafficking from being prosecuted for crimes committed as a direct result of their trafficking situation, first flourished at the state level. These laws underscore a pivotal shift from treating trafficked children as offenders to recognizing them as victims, thus ensuring they receive appropriate support and intervention (Richard, 2004). This victim-centered approach reflects a broader understanding of justice, one that harmonizes with the moral imperatives to protect the innocent and vulnerable, as emphasized in numerous doctrinal teachings.

Furthermore, state legislation often serves as a testing ground for policies that balance the imperative to prosecute traffickers with the necessity of safeguarding human dignity. For instance, states implement various forms of training for law enforcement and public officials, aimed at improving the identification of trafficking victims and ensuring their rights are protected. Such training is crucial for the effective enforcement of laws and embodies a pragmatic application of the principle of subsidiarity, allowing for tailored responses to the unique challenges posed by trafficking in different communities.

However, the disparity in state laws can also present challenges, particularly in terms of jurisdictional conflicts and the consistency of victim services across state lines. The patchwork of legislation means that victims' access to justice and support can significantly vary depending on where they are identified. This inconsistency not only complicates the efforts of law enforcement but also can hinder comprehensive care for survivors, underscoring the need for a more harmonized approach to legislation at the state level (Gulati, 2012).

In conclusion, state-level legislation plays a pivotal role in the broader fight against human trafficking, offering unique insights and innovations that can inform and enhance national efforts. As states continue to evolve and refine their legal frameworks, the potential for more unified and effective strategies against trafficking grows. This ongoing legislative development, underscored by a commitment to justice and human dignity, aligns with the call to action for all members of society to engage in this critical issue.

Prominent State Laws and Their Impact As we delve deeper into the complex tapestry of laws designed to combat human trafficking within the United States, it becomes evident that state-level legislation plays a pivotal role in addressing this grave issue. Each state, with its unique demographic, economic, and political landscape, has adopted various legislative measures to combat human trafficking, reflecting a diverse approach to a universal problem. This exploration seeks to illuminate the significant impact these laws have had on the fight against human trafficking, offering insights into their effectiveness, challenges, and the path forward.

Firstly, it's important to acknowledge the strides made by states like California, which has been at the forefront of enacting comprehensive anti-trafficking laws. The California Transparency in Supply Chains Act, for instance, requires major businesses to disclose their efforts to eradicate slavery and human trafficking from their direct supply chains. This legislation not only promotes corporate accountability but also empowers consumers to make informed decisions, thereby reducing the demand for trafficked labor (Baker, 2012).

Similarly, Texas, with its vast border and significant immigrant population, has implemented stringent laws that enhance penalties for traffickers while providing critical services to survivors. The Texas Human Trafficking Prevention Task Force has been instrumental in coordinating efforts across law enforcement agencies, non-profit organizations, and healthcare providers, demonstrating the potential for multi-stakeholder collaboration in tackling this issue.

On the eastern front, New York has enacted the Safe Harbour for Exploited Children Act, which exemplifies a victim-centered approach. By treating trafficked minors as victims rather than offenders, the law ensures that they receive necessary support and protection, addressing both the immediate and long-term needs of survivors.

The diversity in state-level legislation highlights the adaptive and context-specific nature of the legal responses to human trafficking. However, this variability also presents challenges, particularly in terms of enforcement and inter-state collaboration. Differences in definitions, penalties, and services across states can create confusion and loopholes that traffickers exploit, undermining the fight against trafficking.

Moreover, while many states have made significant progress, others lag behind, lacking comprehensive laws or adequate resources for enforcement and survivor support. This inconsistency not only hampers national efforts but also places undue burdens on states with more robust systems, as they become destinations for traffickers seeking to evade stringent laws elsewhere (Beale, 2018).

Furthermore, the impact of state laws is significantly influenced by the level of public awareness and engagement. Laws are only as effective as the communities that support and enforce them. Public awareness campaigns, education, and community-based initiatives are crucial in creating an environment where trafficking cannot thrive.

Another important aspect is the integration of survivor perspectives in the development and implementation of laws. Survivors' unique insights and experiences are invaluable in crafting effective legislation, identifying gaps in services, and improving enforcement strategies. Their involvement ensures that laws are not only punitive but also restorative and empowering for those they seek to protect.

Additionally, the role of technology in both facilitating and fighting trafficking cannot be overstated. While traffickers utilize the internet and social media to exploit victims, states are increasingly leveraging technology to identify and rescue victims and to educate the public. Innovative solutions such as digital platforms for reporting trafficking, online training for law enforcement, and apps designed to increase awareness and facilitate interventions mark a significant advancement in the legislative toolkit.

The complexity of human trafficking necessitates a holistic approach that encompasses not only legal measures but also socio-economic strategies. State laws must be complemented by policies that address underlying factors such as poverty, inequality, and discrimination, which make certain populations more vulnerable to trafficking.

In conclusion, state laws play a critical role in the fight against human trafficking, with their impact felt across the legal, social, and economic spheres. The diversity of approaches reflects the multifaceted nature of trafficking, requiring tailored, community-based solutions. Yet, challenges remain in ensuring consistency, enforcement, and survivor-centered responses across states. As we move forward, it's imperative that states not only enact comprehensive laws but also foster collaboration, innovation, and public engagement to eradicate human trafficking from our communities.

Chapter 4: Identifying Victims of Human Trafficking

The imperatives to identify victims of human trafficking are deeply embedded in our moral, legal, and societal frameworks. As we turn our gaze towards the markers that can help in identifying these victims, it is crucial to understand that trafficking manifests in various forms, with each victim bearing silent testimony to their exploitation. The signs and symptoms of such exploitation are myriad, woven into the fabric of the victim's daily existence, often obscured by fear and coercion (Nel, 2005).

Indicators of human trafficking encompass a range of physical, emotional, and behavioral cues. Physically, victims might bear marks of abuse or neglect, while emotionally, they may exhibit a spectrum of trauma-related symptoms, including anxiety, depression, or a palpable sense of fear towards authorities or those in positions of power. Behaviorally, victims often have restricted freedom, evidenced by a lack of personal possessions, controlled movement, or an inability to contact family and friends. These indicators, while not exhaustive, provide a framework for identification but require a nuanced understanding to interpret signs that may be hidden in plain sight (Chaffee and English, 2015).

The victim's plight extends beyond their immediate suffering, as their journey towards recovery is fraught with challenges. The path to empowerment and healing is multidimensional, involving legal, psychological, and social support. Recognizing the signs of trafficking is only the initial step in a lengthy process of recovery and rehabilitation, underscoring the need for comprehensive solutions that address the holistic needs of survivors.

Efforts to better identify victims must also contend with the complexities of human trafficking's clandestine nature. Law enforcement, healthcare professionals, educators, and community members play vital roles in recognizing and responding to trafficking, yet their effectiveness is contingent upon their awareness, training, and ability to act compassionately towards victims. It highlights the imperative for continuous education and the development of protocols that place the well-being and safety of the victim at the forefront of the identification process (Butler, 2014).

In conclusion, identifying victims of human trafficking is an essential step towards ending this heinous crime. As a society, fostering an environment where victims can be safely identified and supported is paramount. Through collective vigilance, education, and empathy, we can begin to dismantle the structures that allow human trafficking to thrive, paving the way for justice and healing for the countless individuals whose lives have been irrevocably altered by trafficking.

Signs and Symptoms

Identifying victims of human trafficking is an indispensable first step in the battle against this modern form of slavery. Victims may not always seek help due to various factors such as fear of their traffickers, lack of trust in authorities, or ignorance of their rights. It is, therefore, crucial for society to be vigilant and knowledgeable about the signs and symptoms that may indicate an individual is a victim of trafficking.

One of the most telltale signs of trafficked individuals is their appearance of being controlled or monitored. This can manifest through restricted or controlled communication, where victims are seldom allowed to speak for themselves or are watched closely when they do (Gibbons and Stoklosa, 2016). This behavior is not just a mechanism of physical dominance but also a subtle suggestion of psychological bondage where the victim's spirit and will are tightly harnessed.

Physical signs also play a significant role in identifying victims. Injuries such as bruises, scars, or other marks of physical abuse may be visible indicators. Victims might also show signs of neglect or poor health, a consequence of the harsh conditions they are subjected to (Parenzin, 2020). The body, in its silent testimony, becomes a canvas displaying the historical cruelty it has faced.

The psychological impact of trafficking on victims cannot be understated. Symptoms of anxiety, depression, or post-traumatic stress disorder are common. The mental chains of fear and dependency crafted by traffickers can be even more potent than physical constraints, rendering the victim in a constant state of psychological captivity (Hopper and Hidalgo, 2006).

Victims may also exhibit behaviors indicative of a lack of freedom or autonomy, such as uncertainty in decision-making, fearfulness around authorities, or unfamiliarity with the local language or area. They often possess no personal identification documents, which serves to isolate them further from society and potential avenues of escape (Litam., 2017).

Labor trafficking victims, a subset requiring specific attention, may demonstrate signs unique to exploitation in work environments. For example, they might live in overcrowded, unsafe conditions or seem to owe a debt to their employer from which they cannot escape. Their work conditions often reflect involuntary servitude—long hours with little or no pay, under constant surveillance or threat.

Exploitation in the sex industry presents additional identifiers. Individuals may be branded with tattoos signifying ownership by their traffickers, exhibit signs of physical abuse or sexual assault, or frequent areas known for prostitution with an older, controlling companion.

The manipulation of hope is another dimension traffickers exploit, promising victims a better life or employment opportunities, only to ensnare them into a cycle of abuse and coercion. Recognizing the subtle cues of someone who believed they were embarking on a new life can be instrumental in identifying victims (Hopper and Hidalgo, 2006).

Children, unfortunately, are not spared from this heinous crime. They may display behaviors indicative of sexual exploitation or forced labor, such as possessing expensive gifts without a clear explanation, chronic runaway behavior, or an inability to clarify where they live. In schools, they might exhibit sudden changes in behavior, decline in school performance, or unexplained absences (Plant, 2013).

Identifying victims of human trafficking is a complex and challenging task that requires careful observation and understanding of these diverse signs and symptoms. For devout Catholics, college professors, law enforcement, politicians, lawyers, and life advocates, understanding these indicators is not merely an academic exercise-it's a moral imperative. The fight against trafficking is a testament to our collective humanity, a calling that demands action, compassion, and vigilance(McQuade, 2019).

In conclusion, as we tread on this path of identifying and helping victims of human trafficking, it is essential to approach with a profound sense of responsibility and empathy. The silent cries for help may not always be audible, but with an informed mind and vigilant eyes, we can extend a lifeline to those entangled in the shadows of exploitation. Let us be the beacon of hope and liberation for those who have been denied their fundamental human dignity.

Victim's Plight and the Path to Recovery

The journey of healing and restoration for victims of human trafficking is both profound and precarious. As they emerge from the depths of exploitation, these individuals confront not only the shadows of their past but the luminance of a future yet to be shaped. The distinction between their past and their hopeful progression towards healing is stark, akin to the transition from night to day, each step fraught with its own challenges and triumphs.

Understanding the plight of trafficking victims requires a reflection on the multifaceted nature of their suffering. The psychological, physical, and emotional scars endured are not merely superficial wounds but run deep, affecting the very core of their being. Traffickers often employ manipulative tactics, such as threats, physical abuse, and psychological coercion, to maintain control over their victims, leaving indelible marks on their psyche (Marburger and Pickover, 2020). This manipulation skews the victim's perception of reality, eroding their sense of self-worth and autonomy.

Yet, amidst this darkness, the path to recovery illuminates the resilience of the human spirit. Recovery is not a linear journey but a complex process that necessitates a personalized, holistic approach. It is essential that these individuals receive comprehensive support that addresses not only their immediate needs but also their long-term well-being. This includes access to safe housing, medical care, counseling, legal assistance, and opportunities for education and employment.

Faith-based interventions often play a pivotal role in healing, offering victims not just material support but spiritual nourishment as well. The narrative of redemption and forgiveness found in biblical teachings can provide profound solace and hope to those who have endured the unimaginable. In this context, the act of recovery transcends mere physical and psychological rehabilitation; it becomes a journey of spiritual rebirth and renewal.

However, the societal reintegration of trafficking victims is laden with obstacles. Stigmatization, discrimination, and the lingering effects of trauma can sever their ties to the community, rendering their journey towards normalcy arduous. It is imperative that society cultivates an environment of understanding and acceptance, recognizing survivors not as victims of their past but as bearers of strength and resilience (Hill and Mullins, 2022).

The legal system too plays a crucial role in the survivor's path to recovery. Ensuring traffickers are brought to justice not only affirms the victim's ordeal but also contributes to their sense of closure and empowerment. The Trafficking Victims Protection

Act (TVPA) of 2000 serves as a cornerstone of federal efforts to combat human trafficking and support survivors, outlining provisions for their protection and assistance (U.S. Department of State, 2021).

Yet, the effectiveness of legal and supportive frameworks hinges on their accessibility to survivors. Barriers such as language differences, lack of awareness about available resources, and distrust of authorities can impede victims' access to the help they critically need. Thus, outreach and education efforts must be intensified to bridge these gaps, ensuring that all survivors can navigate the path to recovery with confidence and support.

The role of community and non-governmental organizations cannot be overstated in the recovery process. Through their relentless advocacy, provision of services, and public education efforts, these entities fortify the support network available to survivors. National organizations like Polaris Project and Shared Hope International, alongside faith-based groups such as Catholic Charities and the Sisters of Mercy, exemplify the collective endeavor to uplift trafficking survivors (Polaris Project, 2020).

As survivors embark on their journey to healing, the importance of personal agency and empowerment becomes unequivocally clear. Empowering survivors to make decisions about their recovery process fosters a regained sense of control over their lives, a critical element in overcoming the powerlessness imposed by their traffickers.

Education and employment opportunities serve as powerful tools for empowerment, offering survivors a pathway to self-sufficiency and a means to rebuild their lives. By acquiring new skills and gaining employment, they not only secure their economic independence but also reconstruct their identity beyond that of a victim (Hill and Mullins, 2022).

The story of recovery is one of both individual and collective transformation. It demands a societal shift towards empathy, understanding, and action. Each member of the community, regardless of profession or faith, holds the potential to contribute to this transformative journey. By lending their voice, time, or resources, individuals can play a part in forging pathways of healing and hope for trafficking survivors.

In conclusion, the path to recovery for victims of human trafficking is a testament to human resilience and the power of compassionate intervention. While the road is strewn with challenges, each step forward is a victory against the forces of exploitation and oppression. In their journey, survivors not only reclaim their lives but also illuminate the path for others, serving as beacons of hope and agents of change. Through collective effort and unwavering support, society can aspire to not just mend the wounds of the past but to forge a future where freedom and dignity prevail for all.

Chapter 5: Active Organizations in the Fight

In the concerted effort to eradicate human trafficking, various organizations stand as beacons of hope, illuminating paths toward freedom and recovery. Among these, the Polaris Project and Shared Hope International exemplify the power of national mobilization, seeking not only to rescue victims but also to transform public consciousness about human trafficking (Graw Leary, 2018). Their methodologies, grounded in rigorous data analysis and advocacy, resonate deeply with the ethos of faith-based initiatives like Catholic Charities and the Sisters of Mercy. The latter institutions, fueled by a profound moral imperative, extend their reach to the most vulnerable, providing not just refuge but holistic care that caters to spiritual, physical, and emotional healing. This fusion of secular and faith-based endeavors encapsulates a multifaceted approach to combating human trafficking, reflecting the complex nature of the issue itself. It's through such diversity in strategy and unity in purpose that the fight against human trafficking finds its strength, setting a precedent for engagement and collaboration. Each organization, with its unique capabilities and insights, contributes indispensable parts to the larger mission of dismantling trafficking networks and restoring dignity to survivors. As these active organizations advance in their respective domains, they collectively forge a robust frontline against human trafficking, embodying the virtue of solidarity that

is imperative in this critical fight for human rights and freedom
(Nakamura and Maslow, 2010).

National Organizations

In the ongoing battle against human trafficking, a multitude of national organizations stand on the front lines, wielding knowledge, resources, and dedication to dismantle the chains of oppression. These groups operate across the United States, addressing different aspects of this multifaceted problem, from rescuing victims to advocating for stronger laws. Among them, the Polaris Project and Shared Hope International emerge as beacons of hope, offering comprehensive solutions and support to those ensnared by trafficking's cruel grasp.

The Polaris Project, named after the North Star, that guided slaves to freedom along the Underground Railroad, continues to illuminate the path to liberation for modern-day victims of bondage. By operating the National Human Trafficking Hotline, Polaris serves as a pivotal first point of contact for victims seeking escape and for citizens aiming to report suspicions of trafficking. The organization's data-driven approach empowers policymakers, law enforcement, and community members, equipping them with the necessary tools to enact change (Polaris, 2023).

Similarly, Shared Hope International tackles the scourge of human trafficking through prevention, restoration, and justice initiatives. Founded on the principle that every person deserves freedom, Shared Hope works tirelessly to prevent the conditions that allow trafficking to flourish, restore survivors to their full potential, and bring traffickers to justice. Through its targeted programs and advocacy at both state and federal levels, Shared Hope International makes significant strides toward eradicating trafficking and rebuilding the lives of those affected (Kara, 2006).

It is clear that the intervention of these national organizations is indispensable. They not only provide immediate assistance to victims but also address the systemic issues that perpetuate trafficking. These groups' unwavering commitment symbolizes humanity's potential to conquer even the most daunting challenges. As they confront the darkness of human trafficking with the light of hope and action, society moves one step closer to the day when all individuals can live free from the threat of being bought and sold.

The engagement of every sector of society, including devout Roman Catholics, college professors, law enforcement officials, politicians, lawyers, and life advocates, is crucial in supporting the work of these organizations. By linking arms with these national groups, individuals and communities can contribute to a comprehensive strategy that not only rescues victims but also prevents trafficking from claiming more lives. The collective effort can amplify the impact of national organizations, transforming the fight against human trafficking from a series of isolated skirmishes into a coordinated campaign for freedom and dignity.

In the ongoing battle against the shadows that cast over the liberty and dignity of countless souls, the Polaris Project emerges as a beacon of hope, striving to eradicate the scourge of human trafficking that plagues the modern world. Named after the North Star, historically a guide for those seeking freedom from bondage, this organization embodies the essence of guidance and liberation for individuals ensnared in the chains of modern-day slavery.

Polaris Project: Illuminating the Path to Freedom Through strategic interventions and comprehensive research, the Polaris Project addresses the multifaceted nature of human trafficking. By harnessing data, technology, and direct outreach, Polaris uncovers and disrupts the networks that exploit vulnerable populations. The organization operates the National Human Trafficking Hotline, a lifeline for victims and a crucial resource for law enforcement in identifying traffickers (Polaris Project, 2022).

Human trafficking, a grave violation of human rights, mirrors the injustices that once spurred abolitionists and champions of liberty to action. The Polaris Project, cognizant of the historical and moral imperatives, employs a multifaceted approach to fight trafficking. Their strategies resonate with the principles of justice, freedom, and compassion, echoing the core values emboldened within the teachings of various faith traditions, including the deeply held beliefs of the Catholic Church.

The Catholic Church, with its rich tradition of social teaching, posits that every human being is endowed with an inviolable dignity. This aligns seamlessly with the mission of the Polaris Project, as advocate tirelessly for the inherent worth of every individual. The organization's efforts parallel the Church's call for a society that upholds the sanctity of human life, challenges injustices, and embraces the marginalized. Therefore, the Catholic community, alongside other faith-based entities, finds a profound ally in the Polaris Project against the blight of trafficking.

Crucially, Polaris undertakes research to illuminate the vast, obscured expanse of human trafficking's reach within America. By aggregating and analyzing data, Polaris reveals trends, identifies gaps in the system, and devises targeted interventions. This methodical approach echoes the meticulous scholarship of ancient philosophers who sought to understand the world's complexities through logic and evidence, paving the way for meaningful action grounded in truth.

Moreover, Polaris's philosophy embodies a blend of pragmatism and idealism. They recognize that to dismantle the structures that perpetuate trafficking, collaboration across sectors-government, private industry, and civil society-is essential. This holistic paradigm mirrors the comprehensive worldview of classical thinkers who understood the interconnectivity of social phenomena, advocating for a society harmonized through justice and ethical practice.

Through educating communities, Polaris Project not only spreads awareness but also empowers individuals to become vigilant guardians of their brethren. This educational approach resonates with the biblical injunctions to seek knowledge and wisdom, not solely for personal edification but for the safeguarding and upliftment of one's community. Education, hence, becomes a powerful tool in the arsenal against the forces of darkness that traffic human beings.

The organization's advocacy efforts seek to reform policies and laws to better protect victims and prosecute perpetrators. In navigating the political arena, Polaris employs the art of rhetoric, marshaling compelling arguments and mobilizing public sentiment to effect change. This strategic engagement reminds us of the civic responsibility to wield our voices and influence in the service of justice, a theme recurrent in the discourse of ancient philosophers.

Furthermore, Polaris Project's commitment to victim assistance underscores a recognition of the profound wounds inflicted by trafficking. Offering support services, they embody the scriptural call to comfort the afflicted and to bind up the brokenhearted, reflecting the Gospel's mandate of mercy and compassion towards those who have suffered exploitation and abuse.

One cannot overlook the technological prowess Polaris employs to confront human trafficking. Leveraging innovation to track, analyze, and disrupt trafficking networks, Polaris adapts the wisdom of the ancients to the challenges of the modern age, utilizing the tool of technology not as an end in itself but as a means to advance the cause of justice and human dignity.

In essence, the Polaris Project serves as a modern-day iteration of the classical quest for justice, blending the ancient and the contemporary in its fight against human trafficking. As members of a society yearning for justice, it behooves us to lend our support, whether through advocacy, education, or prayer, to their noble cause.

To the devout Roman Catholics, college professors, law enforcement, politicians, lawyers, life advocates, and all individuals committed to the fight against human trafficking, the Polaris Project offers a model of effective action and moral integrity. It is a call to join hands, across diverse spheres of influence, to uproot the evil of trafficking from our midst.

In conclusion, the fight against human trafficking, epitomized by the endeavors of the Polaris Project, is not merely a contemporary legal or social battle but a deeply spiritual crusade that calls each of us to action. It is an extension of the age-old struggle between light and darkness, a testament to humanity's enduring capacity for both evil and extraordinary goodness. As such, it demands of us a response that is grounded in our deepest philosophical, theological, and moral convictions—a response that affirms the dignity, freedom, and intrinsic worth of every human being.

Shared Hope International emerges as a beacon in the relentless fight against the scourge of human trafficking, endeavoring to dismantle the chains of exploitation through a fusion of advocacy, prevention, and restoration. At its core, Shared Hope International embodies a commitment to restore hope and freedom to the victims ensnared by trafficking's gripping claws.

In our modern age, which prides itself on advancement and enlightenment, it stands as a grievous contradiction that slavery, in its ugliest form, continues unabated. Human trafficking, a blight upon humanity, challenges our moral fabric, urging a response that is both immediate and effective. Hence, the role of organizations like Shared Hope International becomes not just relevant, but critically essential.

The inception of Shared Hope International was inspired by a vision to confront and uproot the horrors of sex trafficking. It acknowledges the profound indignity suffered by the victims and seeks to champion dignity, freedom, and justice. As faith compels action and intellect informs strategy, Shared Hope endeavors to weave together these threads in its approach (Greenbaum et al., 2018).

Their strategies are manifold and meticulously devised. Primarily, the organization focuses on the prevention of trafficking, protection of victims, and the prosecution of perpetrators. This tripartite strategy forms the cornerstone of their mission, mirroring the comprehensive approach needed to combat this multifaceted crime.

Prevention efforts by Shared Hope International are diverse, targeting both potential victims and the wider community through education and awareness programs. These initiatives are grounded in the belief that knowledge is a precursor to freedom, enlightening individuals on the realities of trafficking and empower them to protect themselves and others.

The protection of victims is pursued with a compassion that recognizes their inherent dignity. Shared Hope International provides support for shelters, offers legal advocacy, and facilitates access to medical, psychological, and spiritual care. They strive to meet the complex needs of trafficking survivors, advocating for a path to restoration that respects the individual's journey (Graw Leary, 2018).

Prosecution of traffickers is a critical component of their strategy, aiming to hold perpetrators accountable while dismantling the networks that perpetuate slavery. Shared Hope supports law enforcement training and advocates for robust legal frameworks that equip prosecutors with the tools necessary to bring traffickers to justice.

The organization's commitment to collaboration is evident in its efforts to engage diverse stakeholders, including lawmakers, educators, and faith communities. By mobilizing a collective response, Shared Hope seeks to amplify its impact, fostering a united front against trafficking.

Underpinning all these efforts is a deep-seated belief in the power of hope. Shared Hope International not only works to rescue victims but to restore their dreams and aspirations, illuminating a path forward beyond the darkness of their experiences. This mission is reflective of a profound understanding of human trafficking not only as a legal issue but as a moral crisis.

The success stories of those liberated and restored by Shared Hope serve as a testament to the efficacy of their approach. These narratives do not merely recount tales of survival but underscore the potential for transformation, both for individuals and communities. Yet, the war against trafficking is far from over. The organization continually evolves, responding to emerging trends and challenges in the trafficking arena.

With a firm foundation in Christian values, Shared Hope International harnesses the power of faith as a driving force in the fight against human trafficking. It calls upon the conscience of the global community, advocating for a world where freedom and dignity are afforded to all.

The urgency of this call to action resonates more profoundly in our contemporary society, beckoning every individual to partake in the battle against trafficking. For those entrenched in academia, law enforcement, politics, and faith communities, Shared Hope International exemplifies a model of engagement, illustrating how concerted, informed efforts can dismantle the fortress of slavery.

In conclusion, Shared Hope International stands as a testament to the belief that hope, fortified by action and faith, can indeed triumph over despair. It challenges every segment of society to rise, contribute, and participate in the restoration of freedom, ensuring trafficking's defeat is not a far-off dream but an imminent reality (Kara, 2006).

As we ponder the road ahead, let us draw inspiration from the mission and achievements of Shared Hope International. Their unwavering commitment serves as a clarion call to action, urging us to lend our voices, hands, and hearts in the noble pursuit of a world emancipated from the grip of trafficking.

Faith-Based Initiatives

In the fervent battle against the scourge of human trafficking, a beacon of hope and action shines forth from faith-based organizations, standing as a testament to the power of spiritual conviction melded with practical action. Among these, Catholic Charities and Sisters of Mercy emerge as paradigms of faith in action, channeling their deeply rooted theological beliefs into tangible efforts to combat this modern-day slavery. These organizations not only exemplify the Church's commitment to the dignity of every human being but also mobilize a vast network of resources and volunteers to provide critical services to victims. Leveraging their unique position within communities and backed by a moral imperative, they offer shelter, legal assistance, counseling, and a path to healing and redemption for those ensnared by the dark web of trafficking. Their work stands as a testament to the potential for religious institutions to lead in the fight against trafficking, acting as the hands and feet of a faith that calls for justice, mercy, and liberation for the oppressed (Barrows, 2017). As they wade into the darkness to bring light, these faith-based initiatives embody a profound response to the Gospel's call to love and serve the least among us, proving that spiritual beliefs can fuel practical actions that dismantle the chains of exploitation and despair.

Catholic Charities continues in the vein of compassionate and decisive action against the plague of human trafficking, embodying both the teachings of the Church and the call for justice found within scripture. This organization stands as a beacon of hope, offering shelter, legal assistance, and rehabilitation to victims of this heinous crime. The Church teaches that every human life has inherent dignity, and Catholic Charities puts this belief into action by valuing the life and freedom of every individual ensnared by trafficking.

Integral to understanding Catholic Charities' approach is grasping the breadth of human trafficking's impact across America. While other sections have dealt with defining human trafficking and illustrating the scope of the problem, here we delve into how Catholic Charities intersects with these victims' lives, providing a tangible testament to the commandment of loving one's neighbor as oneself (Hounmenou, 2023).

Human trafficking, in its multifaceted forms, demands a response that is both versatile and robust. Catholic Charities' programs across the country specialize in direct outreach to victims, offering not only immediate support but also long-term assistance for recovery and reintegration into society. This outreach is essential in breaking the cycle of exploitation and offers a lifeline to those who might otherwise have no escape.

Furthermore, Catholic Charities advocates for stronger legislation and policies to protect victims and prosecute traffickers. Their advocacy efforts highlight their commitment to not just assist those in immediate need but also to create a safer and more just society for all. Through engaging policymakers, the organization strives to influence change at a systemic level, echoing the Church's teachings on the common good and the protection of the vulnerable.

The role of Catholic Charities also extends into education and awareness-raising within communities and parishes. Through seminars, workshops, and resources, they strive to illuminate the dark realities of trafficking, equipping individuals and communities with the knowledge to recognize signs of trafficking and respond appropriately. This educational outreach is vital in preventing trafficking and assisting victims, embodying the Church's mission to enlighten and guide its flock.

Another cornerstone of Catholic Charities' work is their collaboration with law enforcement and other social services. Recognizing that human trafficking is a complex issue that no single organization can tackle alone, they foster partnerships that enhance their capacity to serve victims effectively. By working in tandem with civil authorities, Catholic Charities ensures that victims receive comprehensive care that addresses both their immediate needs and their long-term well-being (Lynn, 2021).

Victim support services provided by Catholic Charities encompass a wide range of assistance, from shelter and housing to legal aid and counseling. These services are designed to address the multifaceted needs of trafficking victims, recognizing the trauma they have endured and the challenging road to recovery that lies ahead. Providing a holistic approach to victim support, the organization mirrors the Church's comprehensive understanding of healing and rehabilitation.

In addition to direct support and advocacy, Catholic Charities plays a significant role in mobilizing Catholic communities to act against human trafficking. Through the development and dissemination of resources for prayer, education, and community action, they tap into the vast network of parishes and dioceses to inspire a collective response to this global epidemic.

The theological underpinnings of their work are evident in their commitment to uphold the dignity of every human being, a principle deeply rooted in Catholic social teaching. By addressing the scourge of human trafficking, Catholic Charities manifests the Church's call to uphold the sanctity of life and to work tirelessly for the freedom of those oppressed by modern-day slavery.

It's important to note that while Catholic Charities makes significant strides in combating human trafficking, challenges remain. The hidden nature of trafficking, the fear and trauma experienced by victims, and the constantly evolving tactics of traffickers require that their strategies be adaptive and resilient. However, grounded in faith and driven by a mission to serve, Catholic Charities continues to be a formidable force in the fight against human trafficking, demonstrating the power of faith in action.

Through their comprehensive approach, Catholic Charities not only aids victims but also seeks to address the root causes of trafficking, including poverty, inequality, and lack of opportunity. By tackling these systemic issues, the organization works towards a world where human trafficking is not just addressed after the fact but is prevented from occurring in the first place (Diaz et al., 2021).

The success stories of those who have been rescued and rehabilitated through the efforts of Catholic Charities serve as a testament to the organization's impact. These stories are not just narratives of survival but of renewal and hope, illustrating the transformative power of compassionate intervention and the resilience of the human spirit.

As we continue to confront the evils of human trafficking, the role of organizations like Catholic Charities remains crucial. Their unwavering commitment to the dignity of every person, grounded in the teachings of the Catholic Church, provides not only necessary aid to victims but also a powerful witness to the Gospel's call to love and serve the least among us.

In conclusion, Catholic Charities embodies the Church's response to human trafficking, offering hope, healing, and advocacy for those who have been subjected to this modern-day slavery. Through their tireless efforts, they exemplify the call to action for all of us, urging us to recognize the face of Christ in every victim and to work diligently for their freedom and restoration.

Sisters of Mercy As this chapter unfolds, the significant contributions of faith-based initiatives in combating human trafficking, specifically highlighted in the work of the Sisters of Mercy, come to the forefront. The Sisters of Mercy, a religious congregation of women dedicated to serving those in need, have long been at the frontline of addressing social injustices. Their commitment to eradicating human trafficking is a testament to their unwavering dedication to human dignity and freedom.

In the complex battle against human trafficking, the Sisters of Mercy employ a multi-faceted approach. Recognizing the multifarious nature of trafficking, they engage in education, advocacy, and direct support for victims. Their approach not only addresses the immediate needs of survivors but also aims to tackle the root causes of trafficking, primarily through education and policy change.

Education, both in raising awareness and in offering hope, stands as a pillar of their strategy. By educating communities about the signs and dangers of human trafficking, the Sisters of Mercy empower individuals to become vigilant defenders of their neighbors. They conduct workshops and seminars, often collaborating with schools, parishes, and community groups, to spread knowledge on how to recognize and respond to human trafficking situations (Zhu et al., 2020).

Beyond community education, the Sisters of Mercy are deeply involved in advocacy. They work tirelessly to influence policy at both the national and state levels, advocating for legislation that protects victims and prosecutes perpetrators. Their efforts extend to lobbying for improvements in the support systems for survivors, ensuring they receive the necessary legal, psychological, and social assistance.

Direct support for victims is another critical aspect of their mission. The Sisters of Mercy provide shelter, counseling, and rehabilitation services to help survivors rebuild their lives. Their facilities serve as sanctuaries where victims can find safety, peace, and the opportunity to start anew.

Their holistic approach underlines the conviction that combating human trafficking requires more than just intervention; it demands a commitment to healing and restoration. This conviction is deeply rooted in their faith, which sees every individual as worthy of respect and compassion.

Their efforts have not gone unnoticed. The Sisters of Mercy have established partnerships with law enforcement agencies to better identify and assist victims. These collaborations have enhanced the efficacy of rescue operations and have led to increased prosecutions of traffickers.

In the political arena, the Sisters of Mercy serve as a moral and ethical compass, reminding leaders of their duty to protect the most vulnerable in society. Their advocacy has contributed to the development of more comprehensive anti-trafficking legislation, reflecting a broader understanding of the issue's complexities.

Moreover, their work in the international sphere has highlighted the global nature of human trafficking. The Sisters of Mercy are part of a network of religious and secular organizations fighting trafficking across borders, recognizing that this scourge knows no boundaries (Lynn, 2021).

Their engagement with the public and private sectors in addressing the demand side of human trafficking is another innovative aspect of their work. By raising awareness of how everyday actions can inadvertently support trafficking, they encourage more ethical consumption and business practices.

The Sisters of Mercy also stress the importance of spiritual support for survivors. They offer spiritual counseling and retreats, focusing on healing and forgiveness, which they believe are crucial for full recovery.

Even as they face challenges in their work, including resource limitations and the ever-evolving tactics of traffickers, the Sisters of Mercy persist in their mission. Their resilience is fueled by their faith and the belief that every action counts in the fight against trafficking.

Through their comprehensive approach, the Sisters of Mercy have become a beacon of hope and a model for how faith-based organizations can contribute significantly to society's most pressing issues. Their work exemplifies how compassion, coupled with action, can create ripples of change that extend far beyond their immediate community (Ahn et al., 2013).

The Sisters of Mercy's commitment to ending human trafficking is a powerful reminder of the impact that dedicated individuals and communities can have. It calls on all sectors of society to unite in this cause, leveraging their unique resources and platforms for a traffic-free world.

In conclusion, the work of the Sisters of Mercy in combating human trafficking embodies the principles of mercy, justice, and solidarity. Their multifaceted approach highlights the critical role of faith-based organizations in addressing human rights issues. It serves as an inspiring call to action for all who aspire to contribute to a more just and compassionate society.

Chapter 6: Role of Law Enforcement

Within the intricate battle against human trafficking, law enforcement agencies stand as pivotal guardians of justice, navigating a complex landscape fraught with challenges. Their role transcends the mere application of legal statutes; it embodies a moral duty to safeguard the dignity of every individual ensnared in the shadows of trafficking. The effectiveness of these guardians is often beleaguered by the veiled nature of trafficking activities, rendering the identification and prosecution of perpetrators an arduous task. The inherent difficulties are compounded by the sophisticated networks employed by traffickers to evade detection, challenging law enforcement to adapt continually and innovate in their strategies. Recognizing these hurdles, best practices have emerged, focusing on collaboration with non-governmental organizations, engagement in community policing to foster trust with vulnerable populations, and the deployment of specialized units trained in the nuances of trafficking dynamics (Deeb-Swihart et al., 2019). Furthermore, the development of protocols for victim identification and the integration of victim services within the investigative process have been identified as critical components for not only securing convictions but also for facilitating the healing journey of survivors (Farrell et al., 2008). As guardians of justice, law enforcement's role is dual: to meticulously dismantle the networks of deceit that perpetuate trafficking and to restore the voices of those silenced by exploitation, thereby rekindling the flames of hope and liberation in the hearts of the oppressed.

Challenges in Identifying and Prosecuting Traffickers

The pursuit of justice for victims of human trafficking presents an array of formidable challenges to law enforcement agencies. At the heart of these difficulties are the very nature and mechanisms of trafficking operations, which are designed to operate under the radar of legal scrutiny. These illicit activities are shrouded in layers of deceit, coercion, and manipulation, thereby rendering their unraveling an exceedingly complex task for the authorities.

One of the primary obstacles in identifying traffickers is the covert manner in which they operate. Much like the early Christians navigating the catacombs beneath Rome, trafficking victims and their captors navigate an underworld unseen by the regular populace. These operations often exploit legal businesses as fronts, making the discernment between legitimate operations and criminal enterprises a painstaking process. The use of advanced technology and the dark web for recruiting and advertising victims further compounds the difficulty in tracking and apprehending trafficking rings (Wooditch, 2012).

Moreover, the diverse profiles of traffickers–ranging from organized crime syndicates to family-based operations and solitary individuals–adds another layer of complexity to law enforcement's task. This diversity necessitates a multifaceted approach to training and investigation, requiring resources and expertise that are often in short supply.

Victims' fear and mistrust of authorities further exacerbate the challenge of identifying traffickers. Many victims, conditioned by their captors to fear law enforcement or influenced by previous negative experiences with authorities, may be reluctant to come forward or unable to articulate their experiences. This scenario is reminiscent of biblical tales where fear kept individuals from speaking their truths, underscoring the need for patience, understanding, and compassionate outreach from law enforcement entities.

The global nature of human trafficking also presents significant jurisdictional challenges. Traffickers frequently move victims across state and international borders to evade capture and prosecution, necessitating cooperation and coordination between various jurisdictions and law enforcement agencies. This aspect of trafficking highlights the need for a collaborative approach akin to a unified body of believers, transcending individual capacities to address a collective evil (Berardinis, 2013).

Prosecuting traffickers is further complicated by the demand for concrete evidence, which can be difficult to obtain. Traffickers often go to great lengths to leave no discernable trail, using intimidation or violence to ensure the silence of their victims and associates. The ephemeral nature of digital footprints and the complexity of financial transactions involved in trafficking rings demand sophisticated investigative techniques and tools.

Legal hurdles also pose significant challenges in the fight against human trafficking. Variations in state laws regarding human trafficking can result in inconsistent application of justice and difficulties in prosecuting cases that cross state lines. Furthermore, the reliance on victim testimony – often the pivotal evidence in human trafficking cases – can be problematic given the traumatic impact of trafficking on victims' mental and emotional well-being, affecting their reliability as witnesses.

The interconnection between human trafficking and other forms of crime, such as drug trafficking and cybercrime, presents additional investigative and prosecutorial challenges. These connections necessitate that law enforcement officers have a broad understanding of various forms of criminal activity and the ability to discern complex criminal networks.

Resource constraints further impede the efforts to combat human trafficking. The extensive time and manpower required to investigate trafficking cases strain already limited law enforcement resources. This creates a situation where the immense scope of trafficking operations can overshadow the capacity of investigative teams, necessitating prioritization which might leave some victims without immediate rescue or relief (Farrell et al., 2008).

Public awareness and understanding of human trafficking are crucial to overcoming many of these challenges. Misconceptions about the nature of trafficking and stereotypes regarding victims can hinder investigations and prosecutions. Thus, educating the public to recognize signs of trafficking and encouraging active engagement in reporting suspected trafficking can significantly aid law enforcement efforts.

In conclusion, the journey toward eradicating human trafficking is fraught with formidable challenges, akin to navigating a labyrinth in darkness. It requires unwavering commitment, innovative strategies, and a collaborative spirit among law enforcement entities and the broader community. As this chapter delves into the various hurdles faced in identifying and prosecuting traffickers, it is essential to remember the ultimate goal: to bring light to the darkest corners of humanity and hope to those ensnared by exploitation.

Best Practices and Strategies

As the battle against human trafficking continues, law enforcement agencies stand on the frontline. Their role, pivotal in the eradication of this blight from our society, requires not only dedication but also a strategic and informed approach. The following discourse outlines a series of best practices and strategies that, if adopted, could significantly enhance the efficacy of law enforcement in combating human trafficking.

First and foremost, interagency collaboration emerges as a cornerstone strategy. Given the multifaceted nature of human trafficking, which often spans multiple jurisdictions and even international borders, a collaborative approach amongst various law enforcement agencies is essential. By pooling resources and sharing intelligence, agencies can extend their reach and impact, facilitating a more comprehensive crackdown on trafficking networks (Gulati, 2012).

Training and education within the law enforcement community must also be prioritized. Traffickers often employ sophisticated methods to evade detection, and as such, officers need to be equipped with the knowledge and skills to identify and address these evolving tactics. Specialized training modules that focus on the latest trends in trafficking, victim identification, and the psychological manipulation employed by traffickers can empower officers to act more decisively.

The engagement and partnership with local communities stand as a critical strategy. Trafficking operations often rely on the invisibility afforded by public ignorance or indifference. By fostering strong relationships with community leaders and members, law enforcement can tap into local networks that are likely to notice anomalies indicative of trafficking activities. Such partnerships also pave the way for a supportive environment that encourages victims to come forward.

Utilizing advanced technology and data analysis tools can significantly bolster law enforcement efforts. With traffickers frequently using the internet and social media to recruit and exploit their victims, agencies must harness digital forensic technologies and online monitoring to track and dismantle these digital footprints. Additionally, data analysis can reveal patterns and connections that might otherwise remain obscured, guiding more targeted law enforcement interventions (Richard, 2004).

Victim-centered approaches must be at the heart of law enforcement strategies. Recognizing the complex trauma experienced by trafficking victims, law enforcement personnel must adopt a compassionate and empathetic stance. This involves not only protective custody and care for the victims but also their active involvement in the investigative process, ensuring that their insights and needs inform enforcement actions and strategies.

Embedding law enforcement officers in communities as a proactive measure can also yield dividends. This approach not only enhances the visibility of law enforcement but also its accessibility, fostering an environment where community members feel more comfortable reporting suspicions and crimes. Such a visible presence can act as a deterrent to traffickers considering operating within these communities.

International collaboration is another critical aspect. Human trafficking is a global problem that requires a coordinated global response. By forging partnerships with law enforcement agencies around the world, sharing intelligence, and engaging in joint operations, the capacity to combat trafficking networks that operate across borders is significantly enhanced.

The development and dissemination of standardized protocols for trafficking investigations and victim support can help ensure consistency and quality in the law enforcement response to human trafficking. These protocols can serve as a valuable guide for law enforcement officers, ensuring that they are equipped with the knowledge and tools needed to effectively combat trafficking and support victims (Hendrix, 2010).

Finally, the focus on prevention strategies cannot be underestimated. Law enforcement agencies play a crucial role in prevention efforts, from conducting awareness campaigns that educate the public on the signs of trafficking to engaging with at-risk communities. By preventing trafficking from occurring, law enforcement can save lives and diminish the demand that fuels trafficking networks.

In conclusion, the role of law enforcement in combating human trafficking is multifaceted and challenging. However, through the implementation of best practices and strategic approaches such as interagency collaboration, community engagement, advanced technology utilization, and victim-centered methodologies, significant strides can be made towards eradicating this scourge. It is a moral imperative that law enforcement agencies not only protect the vulnerable but also seek justice for the victims of trafficking, reflecting the core values of compassion and justice that define our society.

Chapter 7: The Political Arena

In traversing the complex landscape of human trafficking, the political arena emerges as pivotal. Here, lawmakers craft the policies that shape the battle against this atrocious crime, with potential pathways toward its eradication resting heavily on the formulation and implementation of cogent, ethically informed laws. Legislation acts not just as a deterrent but also as a reflection of our collective moral compass, illustrating the societal imperative to protect the vulnerable among us. Advocacy, consequently, becomes a linchpin in this domain, a mechanism through which citizens and interest groups can influence policy directions—ultimately, it's about galvanizing political will to confront and dismantle the networks that perpetuate human trafficking. Integral to this advocacy is a nuanced understanding that policy recommendations must balance prevention, protection, and prosecution. Such recommendations may include enhancing support services for survivors, tightening regulations that inadvertently facilitate trafficking, or fostering greater inter-agency collaboration. This chapter, therefore, delves into the intersection of political action and moral imperative, urging a commitment to policies that not only punish the perpetrators but also render visible those hidden in the shadows of our society, thereby affirming the inherent dignity of every individual (Merilainen and Vos, 2015). This conversation sits at the heart of what it means to engage in the political arena against human trafficking-a call to action that transcends partisan lines and speaks to the core of our humanity.

Tackling Human Trafficking Through Policy

As we advance further into the intricacies of the battle against human trafficking, our focus draws nearer to the realm of policy-making. In this domain, the synthesis of moral imperative, legal rigor, and societal action coalesce into a formidable force against the depravities of human exploitation. It is through the vessel of policy that we find our most structured and far-reaching tools for enacting change.

Policy, as it pertains to human trafficking, demands a comprehensive approach that extends beyond the mere prohibition of acts. It entails the crafting of frameworks that not only penalize perpetrators but also provide protection, relief, and rehabilitation for victims. Moreover, it encompasses measures that cut off the financial and operational lifelines of trafficking rings, incorporating strategies for education, prevention, and international cooperation (Ann Stolz, 2007).

In the United States, the seminal Trafficking Victims Protection Act (TVPA) of 2000 stands as a cornerstone of anti-trafficking legislation. It expanded the federal government's tools and resources to combat trafficking, establishing severe penalties for traffickers, and introducing protective measures for victims. However, as trafficking evolves, so too must our policies adapt to confront new challenges and to close the loopholes traffickers exploit (U.S. Department of State, 2001).

State-level initiatives play a critical role as well, given the localized nature of trafficking dynamics. States have the autonomy to tailor legislation and resources to meet the specific needs and circumstances within their jurisdiction. This is evident in the variety and scope of laws passed in different states, from enhancing victim services to stiffening penalties on traffickers.

Yet, legislative progress is often hampered by challenges in implementation and enforcement. The complexities of trafficking cases, combined with a lack of resources and training for law enforcement and judicial bodies, can lead to under-prosecution of traffickers and inadequate support for victims. Therein lies the imperative for policies that not only establish frameworks for justice but also ensure the allocation of necessary resources and training.

Moreover, policy must address the root causes of trafficking, such as poverty, inequality, and corruption, which create a fertile ground for exploitation. Efforts to strengthen education, promote economic opportunities, and foster good governance are thus integral components of a holistic anti-trafficking strategy.

At the international level, the fight against human trafficking necessitates cooperation and collaboration among nations.

Policies must transcend borders, recognizing the transnational nature of trafficking networks. This involves the harmonization of laws, the sharing of intelligence and resources, and the adherence to international standards and protocols.

The role of non-governmental organizations (NGOs) and faith-based initiatives in shaping and supporting anti-trafficking policy is invaluable. These entities often serve on the front lines, offering critical insights into the needs of victims and the mechanisms of trafficking. Their advocacy drives awareness and influences policy, while their services provide a lifeline to those in need (Ann Stolz, 2007).

Within this context, the Catholic Church and other faith communities possess a unique moral authority and expansive network to mobilize against trafficking. The Church's teachings on the dignity of the human person and the evils of exploitation resonate deeply, guiding both congregational action and advocacy efforts at various levels of governance.

Indeed, policy-making is an arena where faith and reason intersect, where moral imperatives inform practical legislation. The commitment to ending human trafficking, grounded in a profound respect for human dignity, calls for policies that reflect both compassion and justice.

Advocacy plays a pivotal role in this regard, galvanizing public and political will towards the enactment and enforcement of effective anti-trafficking policies. It is through the voices of the faithful, the academic, and the professional that the moral urgency to combat trafficking is communicated to those in positions of power.

To this end, the development of policies that tackle human trafficking necessitates a multi-faceted approach, one that involves legislators, law enforcement, NGOs, faith communities, and the public. It is a collective endeavor that requires not only the formulation of laws but also a commitment to their vigorous implementation.

In conclusion, the fight against human trafficking through policy is a testament to what can be achieved when justice, compassion, and action converge. It is a call to all sectors of society to participate in a cohesive and sustained effort to eradicate this scourge, restoring dignity and hope to the most vulnerable among us.

Thus, as we endeavor to weave the ethical threads of our shared humanity into the fabric of policy, let us remain steadfast in our pursuit of justice and unwavering in our compassion for the afflicted. For in this noble quest, we embody the very essence of community and the profound capacity for good that defines us.

Advocacy and Policy Recommendations

The struggle against human trafficking is a battle waged not only on the streets and in the shadows but within the hallowed halls of government as well. It is here, in the political arena, where the fight can be significantly reinforced by informed policy-making and spirited advocacy. This chapter aims to explore an array of policy recommendations that can serve as a beacon for those endeavoring to illuminate and eradicate the dark world of human trafficking.

At the core of our advocacy is the principle that every human being possesses an inherent dignity that must be respected and protected. This conviction aligns closely with foundational moral teachings and has the power to transcend political and religious boundaries, rallying a diverse coalition behind the cause of human freedom.

The first recommendation calls for the enhancement and rigorous enforcement of existing legislation against all forms of human trafficking. Laws like the Trafficking Victims Protection Act (TVPA) have set a significant precedent, yet gaps in enforcement and penalties remain. Strengthening these laws, along with state-level legislation, can deter traffickers while providing justice and support to victims (Merilainen and Vos, 2015).

Another critical area of focus is the implementation of comprehensive training programs for law enforcement and first responders. Recognizing the signs of human trafficking is the first step in preventing and prosecuting this crime. By ensuring that those on the front lines are properly educated, we can significantly increase the identification and rescue of victims.

Education extends beyond law enforcement; there is a pressing need to integrate human trafficking awareness into the curriculum of public education systems. By informing students of the dangers and signs of trafficking, we empower future generations to protect themselves and their peers.

The political arena must also address the demand that fuels the trafficking industry. This involves a multifaceted approach that includes the disruption of online platforms used for trafficking, an increase in sanctions for individuals and entities that are complicit, and public awareness campaigns that highlight the human cost of trafficking.

Furthermore, it is imperative to provide adequate resources for victim recovery. This entails bolstering funding for shelters, counseling, legal assistance, and reintegration programs. Victims of trafficking face a long road to recovery, and a society that values human dignity must be prepared to walk alongside them (Cordisco Tsai, 2022).

International collaboration is another key pillar in the fight against trafficking. No nation stands alone in this battle; it is a global scourge that requires a united response. Strengthening partnerships and sharing best practices can enhance the global community's effectiveness in preventing trafficking, prosecuting traffickers, and protecting victims.

Incentivizing the business community to audit their supply chains for human trafficking is another policy recommendation. By holding corporations accountable for ethical practices, we can reduce the demand for trafficked labor. This effort can be supported by encouraging consumers to patronize companies that prioritize human rights in their operations.

The plight of trafficked individuals must also find a voice in the media. Advocacy for ethical reporting on trafficking issues is crucial. The media holds the power to shape public perception, and responsible journalism can play a significant role in raising awareness and sparking collective action.

At a broader level, policies that address systemic inequalities and vulnerabilities can help to prevent trafficking. For example, economic empowerment programs, accessible education, and support services can eliminate the conditions that traffickers exploit. Health care policies that include screenings for signs of trafficking can also serve as an early intervention tool.

Enhancing legal protections for whistleblowers and survivors who come forward is also vital. Fear of retaliation can silence those who otherwise might speak out. By creating a safe environment for reporting trafficking, we can uncover and address more instances of this heinous crime.

Lastly, the role of faith-based organizations in supporting victims must be recognized and expanded. These groups often serve as a first point of contact for survivors, offering shelter, guidance, and healing. Policies that facilitate the collaboration between government and faith-based services can amplify the support system available to survivors.

As a society, it is our collective responsibility to stand against human trafficking. Through informed policy-making and robust advocacy, we can dismantle the structures that enable this crime and restore dignity and freedom to its victims. The political arena holds the keys to enacting these changes, guided by a moral compass that points unwaveringly toward justice and human dignity.

Chapter 8: Educators' Role in Prevention

In the multifaceted battle against human trafficking, educators occupy a critical frontline position, serving not only as guardians of knowledge but also as vigilant sentinels protecting the vulnerable. The profound impact of education in preempting the reach of traffickers cannot be overstated. It emboldens potential targets with the power of awareness, enlightening students to the murky realities lurking in the shadows of society, while simultaneously nurturing an environment where every child is seen, heard, and valued. Through the incorporation of tailored curricula that address the nuances of human trafficking, educators can foster a culture of vigilance and empathy among the youth. Furthermore, comprehensive training for teachers and administrators is paramount to establish school environments that are not only sanctuaries of learning but also bastions against exploitation (Lemke, 2019).

Integral to this approach is the implementation of programs aimed at equipping educators with the necessary tools to identify warning signs and respond appropriately. Empirical evidence suggests that such educational interventions significantly enhance the ability of school personnel to act decisively in suspected cases of trafficking. As educators stand on the frontline, their unique position enables them to construct bridges between at-risk individuals and the necessary help, thereby disrupting the chain of exploitation. The cultivation of this safeguarding role, through constant vigilance and professional development, embodies a proactive stride toward dismantling the structures that enable human trafficking (Didier and Salas, 2020).

In conclusion, the educators' role in the prevention of human trafficking underscores a collective responsibility to shield the innocence and potential of every child. By interweaving awareness into the fabric of education, schools transform into powerful vanguards of prevention. It's a testament to the idea that knowledge, when wielded with purpose and compassion, can indeed light the darkest corners and guide our youth to safer shores (Farrell, 2011).

Awareness and Curriculum Integration

In our continued journey to dissect the multifaceted roles that contribute to the prevention of human trafficking, we turn our lens towards the realm of education. It's a sector that holds unparalleled power in molding the consciousness of young minds towards societal ills, human trafficking being no exception. Educators, by virtue of their position, can illuminate the dark recesses where ignorance breeds contempt and apathy.

Integrating awareness of human trafficking into the curriculum is not just an option; it's a moral imperative that aligns with the broader educational mission of fostering informed, empathetic, and proactive citizens. This integration can take many forms, from the inclusion of human trafficking topics in social studies, ethics, and health classes to the development of specialized programs that empower students with the knowledge to recognize and respond to trafficking situations (Zhu et al., 2020).

The challenge, however, lies in crafting content that is age-appropriate yet impactful. The gravity and complexity of human trafficking must be conveyed without inducing undue fear or distress. Educators need resources and training to navigate this delicate balance – a task that requires significant support from educational institutions, policymakers, and specialized organizations dedicated to combatting human trafficking.

But why focus on education as a front line in this battle? The answer lies in the transformative power of awareness. Knowledge not only dispels myths and misconceptions surrounding human trafficking but also equips individuals with the tools to recognize potential signs of trafficking and understand their role in prevention. This awareness is a powerful deterrent against the normalization of exploitation and serves as a beacon of hope for potential victims.

Furthermore, curriculum integration fosters a culture of care and vigilance within the school environment. It encourages students to look out for one another and creates an informed community less susceptible to the manipulations of traffickers. Educators can lead by example, demonstrating how vigilance and empathy contribute to the safety and well-being of all community members.

Another dimension to this approach is the empowerment it offers to students. By engaging with the complex issues surrounding human trafficking, students develop critical thinking skills, empathy, and a sense of social responsibility. These lessons go beyond the classroom, equipping students with a moral compass that guides them in making ethically sound decisions throughout their lives (Pooler et al., 2022).

To effectively integrate human trafficking awareness into the curriculum, collaboration is key. Educators should work alongside local law enforcement, human trafficking survivors, and NGOs to provide a comprehensive view of the issue. Such collaborations can also open avenues for guest lectures, workshops, and school-wide awareness campaigns, further embedding the understanding of human trafficking within the school culture.

It's important to note, however, that curriculum integration is not without its challenges. The sensitive nature of human trafficking means that educators must be prepared to handle difficult discussions and offer support to students who may be affected personally by the issue. This necessitates a level of training and preparedness that many educators may not possess without additional support and resources.

Despite these challenges, the push for awareness and curriculum integration is gaining momentum. Success stories from schools that have implemented human trafficking awareness programs serve as a testament to the positive impact of such initiatives. Students emerge not only more informed but also more empowered to contribute to the solution.

In conclusion, the integration of human trafficking awareness into the curriculum represents a critical lever in the fight against trafficking. It embodies the proverbial stitch in time that saves nine, addressing the issue at its roots by cultivating a well-informed and empathetic generation. However, it requires a concerted effort from educators, administrators, policymakers, and community partners to ensure that the approach is not only implemented but sustained.

As we contemplate the future of education's role in combatting human trafficking, let us be guided by the principle that education, in its truest form, is not merely the imparting of knowledge but the shaping of character. In championing awareness and curriculum integration, educators don the mantle of moral custodians, guiding their charges towards a horizon where freedom and dignity are inalienable rights afforded to all.

Now, as we transition from theoretical frameworks to practical applications, our focus shifts towards training educators and school administrators. It is a necessary step to ensure that the vision of an aware, informed, and proactive educational community is not just an ideal but a reality that we can achieve together.

Training Educators and School Administrators

The battle against human trafficking necessitates the involvement of various societal sectors, among which educators and school administrators play a crucial role. It's within the nurturing confines of educational institutions that young minds not only learn about the world but also develop the moral compass to navigate it. Training educators and school administrators thus becomes not just an act of professional development, but a mission imbued with profound ethical significance.

Given the insidious nature of human trafficking, it can often escape the untrained eye. This underscores the imperative need for training programs that equip school staff with the knowledge and tools to identify potential signs of trafficking among students. Such programs aim not only at detection but also at creating an environment where students feel safe to report suspicious activities (Lemke, 2019).

The curriculum for training educators and school administrators must encompass a comprehensive overview of the issue. It should cover the various forms of human trafficking, with an emphasis on those most relevant to children and teenagers, such as labor trafficking, sex trafficking, and the exploitation of youth in traveling sales crews. This knowledge foundation allows educators to contextualize the risk factors and signs they might observe in their students.

Moreover, this educational initiative needs to foster an understanding of the psychological impact of trafficking on victims. Educators, being on the front lines, must be able to approach potentially trafficked students with sensitivity and care, offering a bridge to the professional help they desperately need. This requires training in trauma-informed educational practices, which prioritize the safety, choice, and autonomy of the survivor.

Collaboration with local law enforcement and child welfare agencies is another critical component of this training. Educators and school administrators must know how to navigate the reporting process efficiently and legally, ensuring that suspicions of trafficking are addressed with the urgency and seriousness they demand. This partnership also opens the door to guest lectures and workshops from experts, further enriching the school's knowledge base.

Implementation of this training can take various forms, from seminars and workshops to online courses and modules. It's essential that these training opportunities are made accessible and mandatory for all school personnel, to ensure a unified and informed approach to combating trafficking within educational settings. The creation of dedicated anti-trafficking roles within school staff can also drive further awareness and action.

Pilot programs have demonstrated the efficacy of such training initiatives. Schools that have undergone comprehensive anti-trafficking training report increased confidence among educators in handling suspected cases of trafficking, as well as an uptick in student disclosures of exploitative situations (Didier and Salas, 2020). These outcomes attest to the power of informed, compassionate intervention.

Furthermore, it is crucial that this training not be a one-off event but part of an ongoing professional development plan. The landscape of human trafficking evolves, as do the tactics traffickers use. Regular updates and refresher courses will be necessary to maintain vigilance and adapt strategies accordingly.

Incorporating elements of faith and ethics into the training can also anchor the educators' commitment in a deeper understanding of their role as protectors and guides. Reflection on biblical principles of justice and the inherent dignity of every individual can provide a resilient motivation for educators and administrators in this challenging but vital endeavor.

Lastly, the involvement of survivors in the development and delivery of training materials can offer invaluable insights and foster a more empathetic understanding among school staff.

Their firsthand accounts bring to light the realities of trafficking, challenging stereotypes and misconceptions, and inspiring a diligent and proactive stance against this crime.

The responsibility that educators and school administrators bear in the fight against human trafficking is monumental. By fostering environments that are both vigilant and nurturing, schools can become strongholds against exploitation. Training initiatives are the bedrock upon which this transformative work rests, equipping those at the educational forefront with the knowledge, skills, and heart to stand against trafficking forces (Greenbaum et al., 2018).

In conclusion, as society grapples with the abhorrence of human trafficking, the role of educators and school administrators cannot be overstated. Through comprehensive training, these pivotal figures can illuminate the path to safety for countless unsuspecting victims. It is a call to arms that melds intellectual understanding with moral fortitude, embodying a commitment to the welfare and dignity of every child.

Chapter 9: The Legal Community's Contribution

In the relentless battle against human trafficking, the legal community stands at the forefront, wielding the sword of justice with both precision and compassion. Lawyers and jurists have taken up this noble cause, crafting a bulwark against the darkness through the rigorous prosecution of traffickers and the tender advocacy for victims. Their efforts are not merely acts of professional duty but are deeply rooted in a commitment to uphold the dignity of every human being. Through the meticulous application of existing laws, such as the Trafficking Victims Protection Act (TVPA), legal professionals tirelessly work to ensure that perpetrators of trafficking are held accountable for their crimes, while also forging paths for the restoration and empowerment of those who have suffered at their hands.

Moreover, the legal community acts as a beacon of hope and an agent of change by promoting legal reforms that shore up gaps in current legislation and advocating for policies that prioritize the protection and rehabilitation of trafficking victims (Smith et al., 2021). Legal advocacy groups collaborate with lawmakers, sharing insights gained from the courtroom to shape more effective anti-trafficking laws and policies. Through such collaborative efforts, significant strides have been made in increasing the severity of penalties for traffickers, thereby sending a strong deterrent message. At the same time, legal advocates ensure that the voices of survivors are heard, integrating their experiences and perspectives into legal strategies and policy reforms to combat trafficking more effectively (Nelken, 2010).

Furthermore, the legal community's contribution extends beyond the courtroom and legislative chambers. Through public awareness campaigns and legal education initiatives, lawyers and legal scholars are demystifying the complex legal issues surrounding human trafficking. By educating the public on recognizing the signs of trafficking and understanding the legal remedies available, they are empowering communities to become active participants in the fight against this scourge. As the battle against human trafficking continues to evolve, the legal community's unwavering dedication to justice remains a cornerstone of hope, not only for the restoration of those who have been trafficked but also for the prevention of future crimes (Atkins, 2008).

Prosecuting Traffickers

In the war against human trafficking, the legal community has been called upon as a crucial ally, tasked with the formidable challenge of prosecuting those who perpetrate these grave injustices. Across the landscape of legal battles, prosecuting traffickers is not merely an act of imposing penalties but a profound assertion of human dignity against its desecration. This chapter focuses on the complexities and imperatives of this endeavor, navigating through the intricacies of law, ethics, and societal implications.

The prosecution of traffickers demands a meticulous understanding of both federal and state legislation. The Trafficking Victims Protection Act (TVPA) of 2000 serves as the cornerstone of federal efforts, establishing human trafficking and related offenses as federal crimes. However, laws alone do not suffice. The successful prosecution of trafficker's hinges on the effective enforcement of these statutes, requiring an interwoven effort of local, state, and federal law enforcement agencies.

A critical challenge in prosecuting traffickers lies in the identification and protection of victims. Victims often suffer from profound trauma, making them hesitant to testify against their abusers. It is essential, therefore, that legal proceedings are tempered with compassion and understanding. Victim-centered approaches in the prosecution process not only aid in the healing journey of survivors but also strengthen the case against traffickers by ensuring the availability and credibility of witness testimonies (Nelken, 2010).

Evidence collection in human trafficking cases is fraught with difficulties. The transience of trafficking operations, coupled with the utilization of digital platforms for recruitment and exploitation, necessitates sophisticated investigative techniques. Law enforcement agencies must be adept in cyber investigations and the gathering of digital evidence, as well as traditional surveillance methods.

Another facet of prosecuting traffickers is the imperative of inter-agency and international collaboration. Given the often-transnational nature of trafficking networks, cooperation across jurisdictional boundaries is vital. This involves not only the sharing of intelligence and resources but also the harmonization of legal frameworks and procedural laws to facilitate extradition processes and mutual legal assistance.

The prosecution of human traffickers also brings to the fore the importance of legal advocacy for victims. Legal advocates play a pivotal role in navigating the complex legal landscape, ensuring that victims' rights are protected and that they receive the restitution and justice they deserve. This aspect underscores the necessity of a robust legal support system for survivors, encompassing not just legal representation but also access to social and psychological services.

Moreover, the ethical dimensions of prosecuting human traffickers cannot be overstated. The pursuit of justice must be balanced with the protection of victims' rights and well-being. This ethical consideration mandates a judicious approach to prosecutorial discretion, the deployment of sensitive investigative methods, and the provision of witness protection programs (Aderemi and Adewole, 2022).

Public awareness and education play a critical role in the prosecution of traffickers. A society informed about the signs of trafficking and the legal recourses available can be a formidable ally in identifying and reporting trafficking activities. Community outreach programs and educational initiatives can augment law enforcement efforts by fostering a vigilant public.

Furthermore, sentencing practices for convicted traffickers are a subject of ongoing debate. Adequate sentencing not only serves to punish the perpetrator but also acts as a deterrent to potential traffickers. It is imperative, therefore, that penalties are commensurate with the gravity of the offense, reflecting the severe violation of human rights inherent in trafficking crimes.

The role of prosecutors in this endeavor is both challenging and crucial. They must navigate the complexities of trafficking cases with legal acumen, ethical integrity, and a resolve to uphold justice. Prosecutors are often at the forefront of legal innovations, employing novel legal theories and approaches to hold traffickers accountable.

Legal reforms are also vital to enhancing the prosecution of traffickers. Advocacy for legislative changes to close gaps in existing laws and to introduce measures that facilitate the prosecution process is an ongoing task for the legal community. Such reforms may include provisions for the protection of victims and witnesses, enhancement of penalties, and measures to improve the efficiency of trafficking-related prosecutions.

The cooperation of non-governmental organizations (NGOs) with legal authorities can significantly impact the success of prosecutions. NGOs often play a vital role in supporting victims, raising public awareness, and advocating for policy changes. Their collaboration with the legal system enhances the holistic approach necessary to combat human trafficking effectively.

Finally, the pursuit of justice for victims of trafficking is an abiding testament to the resilience of the human spirit. Each successful prosecution not only brings a trafficker to justice but also restores a measure of dignity to those who were subjected to unspeakable violations. It embodies a collective affirmation that human life is inviolable, and that society will not tolerate its commodification.

In conclusion, prosecuting traffickers is a multifaceted challenge that demands a concerted effort from the entire legal community and society at large. It is a calling that requires not only technical legal expertise but a deep commitment to justice, compassion, and human rights. As this crucial work continues, it is the hope and endeavor of all involved to see a world where human trafficking is eradicated, and freedom and dignity prevail for all.

Legal Advocacy for Victims

In the labyrinth of human suffering that trafficking embodies, the legal community emerges as a beacon of hope, championing the cause of those ensnared. Legal advocacy for victims is not just a matter of navigating the court system; it is the ethical duty to restore dignity and rights to individuals who have been stripped of their autonomy. This responsibility involves not only prosecuting traffickers but also ensuring that the victims receive the support and recognition necessary to rebuild their lives.

The first step in legal advocacy is acknowledging the complexity of the legal challenges faced by victims. Trafficked individuals often find themselves ensnared in a web of legal issues that extend beyond the immediate criminal acts of their traffickers. These can include immigration complications, custody disputes, and the need for protective orders, among others. A comprehensive legal strategy must, therefore, address both the criminal and civil legal needs of the victim.

One significant area of advocacy involves assisting victims with their legal status. Many victims, especially those trafficked from abroad, may not have legal permission to stay in the country. The Trafficking Victims Protection Act (TVPA), established in 2000, introduced measures such as the T visa, which permits victims of trafficking to remain in the United States and eventually apply for permanent residency if they assist in the investigation or prosecution of their traffickers (U.S. Department of State, 2020). Legal advocates play a crucial role in navigating these complex immigration processes on behalf of the victims.

Another critical function of legal advocacy is the pursuit of restitution and compensation for victims. The detrimental impact on a victim's life-physically, emotionally, and financially-cannot be overstated. Legal advocates work tirelessly to ensure that victims receive restitution from their traffickers, as well as exploring other avenues for compensation, such as victim compensation funds or civil lawsuits against perpetrators and, in some cases, negligent third parties.

Victim-witness advocacy is another cornerstone of legal advocacy. Navigating the criminal justice system can be a daunting and traumatic experience for victims. Legal advocates serve as liaisons between the victims and the prosecutors, providing support during interviews and trials, and ensuring that the victims' rights are upheld throughout the criminal justice process.

Confidentiality and privilege issues present unique challenges in legal advocacy. Given the sensitive nature of trafficking cases, preserving the confidentiality of the victims is paramount. Legal advocates must navigate these issues carefully, ensuring that communication with their clients is protected while adhering to legal standards and obligations (Nelken, 2010).

Policy advocacy is another critical aspect, as legal advocates work to influence and reform laws and policies at the state and federal levels to better protect and serve trafficking victims. This includes efforts to streamline the legal processes for obtaining T visas, increasing funding for victim services, and ensuring that anti-trafficking laws are comprehensive and effectively enforced.

Training and education form the bedrock upon which effective legal advocacy rests. Legal professionals must be equipped with a deep understanding of the nuances of human trafficking laws and the unique needs of trafficking victims. This includes ongoing education on new laws, policies, and best practices in victim advocacy.

Collaboration with other professionals is indispensable in the fight against trafficking. Legal advocates often work in tandem with law enforcement, social services, health care providers, and other stakeholders to ensure a coordinated and comprehensive response to trafficking cases. This multidisciplinary approach ensures that victims receive the holistic support they need to heal and rebuild their lives.

The role of faith-based and community initiatives in supporting legal advocacy cannot be understated. These organizations often provide essential services, such as housing, counseling, and employment assistance, that complement the legal support victims receive. Furthermore, they can play a pivotal role in raising awareness about human trafficking and mobilizing community support.

The vicarious trauma experienced by legal advocates working in the human trafficking field is an issue that requires attention and support. The emotional toll of engaging with the profound suffering of victim's day in and day out can lead to burnout and secondary traumatic stress. Providing mental health and wellness support for advocates is vital in sustaining the legal community's efforts against trafficking.

The journey of legal advocacy is fraught with challenges but punctuated by moments of profound triumph. Each case won represents not just a legal victory but a significant step toward justice and healing for the victim. Legal advocacy, therefore, is not just an occupation; it is a calling to stand in solidarity with those who have been marginalized and silenced.

The role of legal advocacy in the broader fight against human trafficking is both critical and multifaceted. From securing justice and reparations for victims to influencing policy and legislation, legal advocates play an indispensable role in disrupting the cycles of exploitation and abuse. It is a testament to the power of the legal profession in effecting tangible, positive change in society.

In conclusion, the legal community's contribution to combating human trafficking through victim advocacy underlines the profound impact that legal professionals can have on individuals' lives and society as a whole. As the fight against human trafficking continues to evolve, the commitment and dedication of legal advocates remain unwavering, driven by a pursuit of justice, human dignity, and freedom for all.

Chapter 10: Technological Frontiers Against Trafficking

As we traverse further into the heart of this discourse, we uncover the profound symbiosis between technology and the combat against human trafficking. In an era where the internet and social media platforms have become double-edged swords-serving both as tools for traffickers and mechanisms for liberation-the pursuit of innovative solutions has never been more critical. The backbone of this chapter delves into how surveillance and monitoring of online domains have facilitated a remarkable leap in identifying and rescuing victims (Muraskiewicz and Vacoula, 2016). It's an epoch of digital vigilantism, where algorithm-based solutions and machine learning techniques are harnessed to detect patterns and signs of trafficking activity, offering a semblance of hope amidst the digital chaos. Additionally, the emergence of victim identification technologies portrays a beacon of light, providing unprecedented assistance in pinpointing and aiding those ensnared by trafficking networks. This narrative isn't merely about the harnessing of digital frontiers; it's a testament to human resilience and intellectual prowess, leveraging the very fabric of technological evolution to safeguard the sanctity of human dignity and freedom (Landron, 2021). Such advancements not only underscore a significant shift in the battlefield against trafficking but also illuminate the path for future endeavors aimed at eradicating this blight from humanity. As we immerse ourselves in these technological frontiers, it's imperative to balance innovation with ethical considerations, ensuring that our zeal for progress does not overshadow the respect for individual privacy and rights, thus embodying the virtues of justice and compassion that form the cornerstone of our collective ethos (Bean, 2016).

Internet and Social Media

In the contemporary epoch, the digital realm, encompassing the internet and social media, has emerged as a double-edged sword in the arena of human trafficking. On one flank, it facilitates traffickers in the covert advertisement of their illicit services and the ensnarement of unsuspecting individuals through deceptive online personas and promises. A study by Landron (2021) delineates how the digital age has furnished traffickers with unprecedented mechanisms for manipulation and control, effectively transforming the physiognomy of exploitation. Conversely, this digital expanse also presents a fertile ground for innovation and vigilance in the crusade against this heinous crime.

Among the armamentarium against trafficking, surveillance and monitoring tools have burgeoned, leveraging artificial intelligence and data mining to detect patterns indicative of trafficking activity online. Initiatives such as the development of algorithms capable of sifting through vast expanses of internet data to identify potential trafficking scenarios exemplify the progressive melding of technology and humanitarian resolve. Furthermore, social media platforms, once critiqued as avenues for exploitation, are now being reconceived as bastions of awareness and community mobilization.

The imperative role of collaboration between technological firms and law enforcement cannot be understated. The synergy of these entities in harnessing digital tools for the surveillance of trafficking activities engenders a proactive rather than reactive approach to trafficking. Enhanced cooperation is fostered through mechanisms such as the sharing of digital footprints related to suspected trafficking rings and the utilization of social media analytics to unveil networks of exploitation (Muraszkiewicz and Vavoula, 2016).

Yet, this emergent frontier is not devoid of ethical quandaries. The vanguard of privacy concerns vis-à-vis surveillance, and the potential for misuse of monitoring technologies, underscores the necessity for a judicious balance between vigilance and the protection of individual liberties. The discourse must gravitate towards developing frameworks that uphold human dignity while emboldening efforts to dismantle trafficking networks. This delicate equilibrium seeks to embody the principle that technological advancement should not outpace the moral compass guiding its application.

In conclusion, the nexus of internet and social media within the context of trafficking elucidates a terrain rife with both perils and promise. As the digital domain continues to evolve, so too must the methodologies employed to confront trafficking. This dynamic calls for continuous reflection, innovation, and above all, an unwavering commitment to the preservation of human dignity. Through the concerted efforts of all societal sectors—be they governmental, technological, or civil—the scourge of trafficking can be confronted more effectively in the digital age.

Surveillance and Monitoring As we venture deeper into strategies employed in the battle against human trafficking, we find ourselves at the confluence of technology and vigilance. It is within this domain that surveillance and monitoring emerge as critical tools, harnessing the power of the internet and social media to both identify victims and apprehend traffickers. However, this endeavor is not without its ethical quandaries and challenges, necessitating a conversation grounded in prudence, justice, and respect for human dignity.

The digital age, while a beacon of progress, has inadvertently become a facilitator for the darker aspects of humanity, including human trafficking. Traffickers adeptly exploit the anonymity and vast reach of the internet to recruit, exploit, and control their victims. Recognizing this, law enforcement agencies, alongside technological innovators, have begun to wield the very tools used by these malefactors to thwart their actions. This entails sophisticated surveillance mechanisms and monitoring systems aimed at detecting online activities related to trafficking.

At the forefront of this fight is the development and application of algorithms capable of scouring the internet's expansive networks to identify patterns indicative of trafficking activities. These algorithms search through advertisements, social media posts, and online forums, looking for signs that might suggest exploitation. Remarkably, such technology has been instrumental in rescuing victims and dismantling trafficking networks, demonstrating the potential of technological interventions in this arena.

However, the employment of surveillance and monitoring for the purpose of combatting human trafficking raises significant ethical considerations. The balance between protecting individuals from harm and respecting their privacy and rights is delicate. It is a testament to our collective moral responsibility to ensure that in our endeavor to protect the vulnerable, we do not inadvertently infringe upon the liberties and privacies that are foundational to a just society.

The Catholic Church, with its rich social teaching, emphasizes the inherent dignity of every human person and the necessity of the common good. In this light, the Church supports efforts to eradicate human trafficking, advocating for the use of technology as a tool for good, so long as it respects the dignity of individuals and promotes justice. It is this ethical framework that must guide the development and deployment of surveillance and monitoring technologies in the fight against trafficking (Lee, 2013).

Moreover, the effectiveness of these technological tools depends heavily on the cooperation between various stakeholders. Law enforcement agencies, tech companies, non-governmental organizations, and communities must work in tandem, sharing information and resources to enhance the effectiveness of monitoring efforts and ensure the protection of human rights.

One of the significant challenges in the use of surveillance and monitoring to combat human trafficking lies in the adaptability of traffickers. As authorities evolve their strategies, so too do those engaged in trafficking, finding new and covert methods to evade detection. This dynamic necessitates continuous innovation and vigilance, requiring resources and commitment from both the public and private sectors.

Additionally, there is the challenge of ensuring that the use of technology does not lead to a surveillance state. The tools developed to combat trafficking must be carefully regulated, with clear guidelines and oversight to prevent abuse. Advocacy for policies that safeguard privacy while enabling effective monitoring is critical in this context.

An interesting development in the realm of surveillance and monitoring is the increasing involvement of the public in reporting suspected trafficking activities. Smartphone applications and online platforms have been developed, enabling citizens to report anonymously signs of trafficking, thus widening the net of surveillance through community engagement. This approach not only aids in the identification and rescue of victims but also fosters a culture of vigilance and responsibility among the populace.

While the focus on technological solutions is paramount, it's essential to recognize that technology alone cannot solve the issue of human trafficking. Comprehensive approaches that include education, economic empowerment, and legal reform are crucial. Surveillance and monitoring, while powerful tools, are part of a broader strategy that requires multidimensional efforts to address the root causes of trafficking and protect those most vulnerable.

As we look to the future, the potential of artificial intelligence and machine learning in enhancing surveillance and monitoring capabilities offers hope. These technologies could provide even more nuanced and effective tools for identifying trafficking activities and assisting victims. Nevertheless, as we harness these advancements, the ethical considerations and the need for a human-centered approach remain paramount.

In conclusion, surveillance and monitoring represent significant strides in the fight against human trafficking. Through ethical application and collaboration among all sectors of society, these tools can shine a light on the dark corridors of trafficking networks, rescuing victims and bringing perpetrators to justice. In this endeavor, we are called to wield technology with wisdom, ensuring that our fight against trafficking upholds the dignity of all individuals and strives for the common good.

Our commitment to combating human trafficking through the prudent use of surveillance and monitoring reflects our broader commitment to justice, mercy, and the inherent dignity of every human person.

Innovation in Victim Identification

In the struggle against human trafficking, the coupling of human insight with technological advancements has paved new roads for identifying victims hidden in plain sight. Much like the lamp beneath the bushel, victims of trafficking often remain obscured by the shadow of societal ignorance and technological limitation. However, as we venture deeper into the technological frontiers against trafficking, a beacon of hope emerges through innovation in victim identification.

One of the most transformative tools in this arena is artificial intelligence (AI), which, through its capability to analyze vast datasets, can reveal patterns and connections that might elude human observers. AI algorithms have been developed to scour the internet, especially social media platforms and the dark web, where traffickers frequently operate. By detecting anomalies in online behavior or identifying imagery that matches known indicators of trafficking, these algorithms serve as the modern-day equivalent of the Biblical watchman, vigilant on the walls of our digital cities (Nel, 2005).

Facial recognition technology further enhances our capacity to locate victims. Once a tool for unlocking smartphones or tagging friends in social media posts, facial recognition has evolved into a critical asset in tracing the movements of missing persons, some of whom are hidden within the depths of trafficking networks. When integrated with surveillance systems across airports, hotels, and public spaces, facial recognition can flag individuals previously reported as missing or at risk, aiding in their rescue and the apprehension of their captors (Chaffee and English, 2015).

A lesser-known yet potent tool in victim identification is linguistic analysis software, which evaluates online advertisements and communications for patterns consistent with trafficking scenarios. This technology delves into the subtle nuances of language, detecting indicators of coercion or exploitation. Its precision mirrors the discernment advised in scriptural wisdom, allowing us to separate the wheat from the chaff in vast fields of digital information.

Blockchain technology, renowned for its security and transparency, offers a novel approach to safeguarding victim identities while ensuring the integrity of evidence collected during trafficking investigations. Through its decentralized ledger, blockchain can securely store encrypted data from victim interviews, surveillance footage, and digital footprints left by traffickers, thereby bolstering legal cases against perpetrators while protecting victim identities from retaliation.

Collaboration across sectors amplifies the impact of these technological innovations. Partnerships between technology firms, law enforcement agencies, and non-governmental organizations have led to the development of platforms where information on suspected trafficking activities can be shared swiftly and securely. This synergy not only hastens the identification and rescue of victims but also embodies the collective action called for in addressing the moral blight of human trafficking.

Despite these advances, challenges remain. The ethical considerations surrounding surveillance technologies, AI, and facial recognition are subjects of intense debate. Concerns about privacy, consent, and the potential for misuse necessitate a balanced approach, ensuring that the pursuit of justice does not encroach upon the dignity and freedom of individuals. This balance requires wisdom and discernment, virtues extolled in both sacred texts and philosophical treatises, guiding us toward ethical action in the digital age.

Moreover, the dynamic nature of trafficking networks, which evolve in response to law enforcement tactics, means that technological innovations must be continuously refined and updated. It's a perpetual game of cat and mouse, where vigilance and adaptability are paramount.

Public awareness and education play a crucial role in this technological ecosystem. As individuals become more informed about the signs of trafficking and the tools available for reporting suspected activities, the collective capacity to identify and assist victims grows exponentially. This societal engagement is akin to the call for communal responsibility seen in parables and teachings across cultures and religions.

Looking forward, the integration of virtual and augmented reality into training programs for law enforcement and public servants offers promising avenues for enhancing the identification of trafficking scenarios. By simulating real-world environments and situations, these technologies can improve the ability of individuals to recognize and respond to the subtle cues of trafficking, strengthening the front lines of defense against this heinous crime.

The role of data privacy laws and regulations in shaping the use of technology in victim identification cannot be overstated. As lawmakers grapple with the implications of emerging technologies, the creation of legal frameworks that both enable effective victim identification and protect individual rights is crucial. Herein lies a call to action for policymakers to navigate these complex issues with wisdom and foresight.

The path forward demands a multifaceted approach, combining technological innovation with ethical consideration, cross-sector collaboration, and continuous education. As we harness the vast potential of technology in the service of human dignity, we embody the collective quest for justice that transcends religious, cultural, and national boundaries (Butler, 2014).

In conclusion, innovation in victim identification stands as a testament to human ingenuity's capacity to confront the scourge of trafficking. Through the considered application of technology, collaboration across disciplines, and adherence to ethical principles, we forge a future where freedom prevails over exploitation. In this endeavor, we echo the age-old aspiration for liberation, recalling the profound words that have inspired generations: "Let my people go."

Chapter 11: International Collaboration

In the relentless fight against human trafficking, the role of international collaboration cannot be understated. It is through the combined efforts of nations that we find the strength to address this pervasive evil that knows no borders. Partnerships for prevention, as highlighted in this chapter, demonstrate a united front that leverages global organizations and agreements to combat human trafficking (Foot, 2020). These alliances bring together the expertise, resources, and authority needed to dismantle trafficking networks and provide justice and healing for victims. For instance, the collaboration between UN agencies and NGOs offers a strategic approach to policy advocacy, victim support, and perpetrator accountability. Such cooperative endeavors signify hope in the darkness, echoing the Biblical call to "defend the oppressed, take up the cause of the fatherless; plead the case of the widow" (Isaiah 1:17, NIV). The importance of these partnerships in spearheading initiatives that span across continents cannot be overstated, as they enable the enactment of comprehensive strategies that target the roots and branches of human trafficking. Through global collaboration, we not only share the burden of combat but also the vision of freedom and restoration for all God's children, encapsulating a universal call to action that transcends cultural and political divides.

Partnerships for Prevention

In the concerted effort to combat the grievous sin and crime of human trafficking, the necessity of international collaboration cannot be overstated. As articulated within the framework of our global society, the malaise of trafficking is not confined by political or geographical boundaries. It thrives in the dark corners of our interconnected world, exploiting the vulnerable across nations. It is within this context that 'Partnerships for Prevention' emerges as a beacon of hope, underscoring the axiom that in unity, there is strength. Drawing upon principles of compassion, justice, and solidarity, such partnerships represent the confluence of diverse efforts aimed at eradicating this blight upon humanity.

At the heart of these collaborations are global organizations and agreements that serve as the linchpins in the international endeavor against trafficking. Agreements such as the United Nations Protocol to Prevent, Suppress and Punish Trafficking in Persons, Especially Women and Children, complement regional and bilateral treaties, creating a robust legal framework. These accords facilitate extradition, mutual legal assistance, and the sharing of best practices among nations (United Nations, 2000). Yet, beyond the legal instruments, these partnerships foster a spirit of cooperation that transcends mere compliance with laws. They embody a shared moral imperative to uplift the dignity of every human being, echoing the universal call to "act justly, love mercy, and walk humbly with your God" (Micah 6:8).

The efficacy of such international partnerships is amplified through the engagement of non-governmental organizations, faith-based groups, and civil society. These entities bring to the table a wealth of experience, resources, and, most critically, grassroots connections that are indispensable in the fight against trafficking. For instance, organizations like the International Justice Mission work alongside local law enforcement in various countries to rescue victims and prosecute traffickers, demonstrating the tangible impact of collaborative efforts (International Justice Mission, 2021). Similarly, faith-based initiatives leverage their extensive networks and moral authority to provide care for survivors and advocate for systemic change, embodying the scriptural mandate to "defend the weak and the fatherless; uphold the cause of the poor and the oppressed" (Psalm 82:3).

However, for these partnerships to realize their full potential, a multifaceted approach is imperative. This involves not only proactive measures to prevent trafficking and protect victims but also strategies aimed at addressing the root causes of vulnerability, such as poverty, inequality, and discrimination. Education and public awareness campaigns play a crucial role in this regard, empowering communities to recognize and resist the mechanisms of trafficking. Additionally, economic empowerment initiatives offer survivors and at-risk individuals viable alternatives to exploitation, thereby breaking the cycle of vulnerability.

As we contemplate the road ahead, it is clear that the battle against human trafficking requires a sustained and cooperative effort. While challenges remain, the progress achieved through international partnerships offers a testament to the power of collective action. Guided by a moral compass that values every human life, we are called to widen the circle of compassion and cooperation, forging alliances that transcend borders in the pursuit of a world free from the scourge of trafficking.

Global Organizations and Agreements As we delve deeper into the mechanisms of international collaboration in the relentless fight against human trafficking, we must recognize the pivotal role played by global organizations and agreements. These entities not only foster cooperation among nations but also standardize approaches to combatting trafficking, ensuring that efforts are not fragmented or isolated. This chapter seeks to illuminate the labyrinth of international networks and treaties that stand as our collective bulwark against the scourge of human trafficking.

The United Nations, through its Office on Drugs and Crime (UNODC), has been at the forefront, spearheading efforts with the Protocol to Prevent, Suppress and Punish Trafficking in Persons, especially Women and Children, also known as the Palermo Protocol. This landmark treaty, part of the larger UN Convention against Transnational Organized Crime, offers a comprehensive definition of human trafficking and lays down the blueprint for the criminalization of all forms of trafficking (United Nations, 2000).

Beyond establishing definitions, the Palermo Protocol emphasizes the 'three P's' strategy: Prevention, Protection of victims, and Prosecution of traffickers. It is the adherence to these principles that guides the international community's response to trafficking, ensuring that efforts are not solely punitive, but also aimed at rehabilitation and root cause eradication.

Another pivotal entity in this global fight is the International Labour Organization (ILO), which focuses on the eradication of forced labor and child labor — two critical components of human trafficking. Through conventions such as the Forced Labour Convention (No. 29) and the Worst Forms of Child Labour Convention (No. 182), the ILO sets international labor standards that combat the economic underpinnings of trafficking (International Labour Organization, 1930, 1999).

The role of regional coalitions cannot be understated, as they provide a tailored response that considers cultural, economic, and political nuances unique to each region. The European Union, for instance, adopted the Directive 2011/36/EU on preventing and combating trafficking in human beings and protecting its victims, which harmonizes anti-trafficking laws across member states, ensuring a unified response within Europe (European Parliament & Council, 2011).

In Africa, the African Union's Ouagadougou Action Plan to Combat Trafficking in Human Beings, Especially Women and Children, exemplifies a continent-wide commitment to address trafficking by enhancing cooperation and adopting comprehensive measures focused on prevention, protection, prosecution, and partnership (African Union, 2006).

The Americas are not left behind, with the Organization of American States (OAS) adopting the Work Plan against Trafficking in Persons in the Western Hemisphere. This plan focuses on strengthening the capacities of member states to prevent and combat trafficking, with a special emphasis on protecting victims and promoting their rights.

These frameworks, agreements, and organizations are instrumental in fostering an environment of cooperation, sharing best practices, and ensuring that nations do not combat trafficking in isolation. International collaboration facilitates the exchange of intelligence, bolsters legal and law enforcement frameworks, and enhances victim support systems across borders.

However, the efficacy of these global agreements and organizations is contingent upon the commitment and action of individual member states. National laws must be aligned with international standards, and countries must invest in the infrastructure and resources necessary for these frameworks to translate into tangible results on the ground.

Moreover, the spiritual and moral dimensions of this fight cannot be overlooked. Trafficking, at its core, is an egregious violation of human dignity, a principle that is paramount in many faith traditions, including Catholicism. The Catholic Church, with its extensive global presence and moral authority, plays a crucial role in raising awareness, advocating for victims, and supporting anti-trafficking efforts both at the grassroots and international levels.

As we navigate this complex landscape of global organizations and agreements, it's imperative that all stakeholders, from governments to faith communities and civil society, work in concert to eradicate human trafficking. The fight against trafficking is not merely a legal or political challenge but a moral imperative that calls for a unified, global response rooted in the principles of human dignity and freedom.

Within this collaborative framework, there's room for every individual to contribute — from those formulating policies to those on the front lines providing shelter and rehabilitation to victims. Our collective action, informed by empathy and justice, can forge a future where human trafficking is relegated to the annals of history.

In conclusion, as we reflect on the role of global organizations and agreements in combatting human trafficking, it's clear that while significant strides have been made, the journey ahead remains daunting. The fabric of international cooperation, woven through treaties and organizations, provides the structure within which this grave injustice can be combatted. Yet, it is through our shared humanity, underpinned by faith and moral courage, that we will ultimately prevail in this fight.

Chapter 12: Community Efforts and Volunteerism

In our collective endeavor to eradicate the blight of human trafficking from our communities, it becomes imperative to galvanize local efforts and foster a culture of volunteerism. At the heart of such community-driven missions is the understanding that each individual, irrespective of their vocation-be it in academia, law enforcement, legal fields, politics, or within the sanctity of religious life-holds a pivotal role in the battle against this heinous crime. By leveraging grassroots activism, communities can cultivate a vigilant and responsive environment that preemptively identifies and aids victims while staunchly opposing traffickers (Leventhal, 2019). Support networks spearheaded by volunteers offer tangible resources and emotional solace to those rescued from the clutches of trafficking, facilitating their journey towards healing and integration into society. Furthermore, the strength of community bonds becomes a bulwark against the isolation often exploited by traffickers. Empirical studies underscore the efficacy of localized, volunteer-led initiatives in not only providing immediate assistance to victims but also in nurturing an ethos of vigilance that deters traffickers. Thus, the mosaic of community efforts, underpinned by a spirit of volunteerism, emerges as a formidable force in the broader tapestry of anti-trafficking strategies, echoing the biblical mandate to "love thy neighbor as thyself" in profound and practical ways.

Grassroots Activism

In our journey through the multifaceted battle against human trafficking, we encounter the vibrant and essential realm of grassroots activism. At the heart of community efforts and volunteerism, grassroots activism embodies the collective power of individuals united by a shared vision of justice and human dignity. It's a testament to the belief that every voice matters and that change, often monumental, begins with the smallest of steps.

Grassroots activism draws its strength from the local level, leveraging the unique insights, passions, and capabilities of community members. It operates on the premise that those most familiar with their community's nuances are best positioned to identify its vulnerabilities to human trafficking. Through awareness campaigns, education, and direct action, grassroots activists work tirelessly to illuminate the dark corners where trafficking thrives.

Community-led initiatives often serve as the first line of defense against human trafficking. They create safe spaces for dialogue, where the stigma surrounding the issue can be dismantled and survivors can share their stories. Here, the importance of narratives cannot be overstated, as they bridge the gap between statistics and the human experience, fostering a deeper understanding and empathy within the community.

The mobilization of grassroots efforts can take many forms, from awareness walks and fundraisers to the formation of local watchdog groups. Such activities not only raise the profile of human trafficking within the community but also generate vital funds that support victim recovery programs and preventive measures (Foot, 2020).

Another critical aspect of grassroots activism is its role in policy advocacy. Armed with firsthand knowledge of trafficking's impact, activists lobby for legislation that enhances victim support services, strengthens law enforcement's ability to prosecute traffickers, and promotes educational programs that target at-risk populations.

Collaboration is the lifeblood of effective grassroots activism. By forging partnerships with schools, faith communities, law enforcement, and other stakeholders, activists create a cohesive network that amplifies their message and extends their reach. This unity in diversity marks the convergence of various perspectives, skills, and resources, all harnessed towards a common goal.

Grassroots activists also serve as watchdogs, holding institutions and officials accountable for their roles in either combating or inadvertently perpetuating trafficking. Through persistent advocacy and public education, they exert pressure on policymakers and corporate entities, demanding transparency, accountability, and a commitment to ethical practices.

The impact of grassroots activism is not limited to prevention and direct action; it also plays a pivotal role in shaping societal attitudes towards victims of human trafficking. By challenging stereotypes and dispelling myths, activists foster a culture of compassion and understanding that transcends judgment and stigma.

Education is a cornerstone of grassroots efforts. Workshops and seminars aimed at equipping individuals with the knowledge to recognize and respond to signs of trafficking are central to mobilization. Here, the power of information becomes apparent, as enlightened citizens transform into vigilant guardians of their community.

Volunteerism is the engine that drives grassroots movements. The selfless dedication of volunteers, who often balance activism with their personal and professional lives, is a beacon of hope and humanity. Their commitment exemplifies the profound impact of collective action, serving as an inspiration to others to join the cause.

The digital age has afforded grassroots activism new platforms and tools, expanded its reach and facilitated the sharing of resources, strategies, and success stories. Social media, in particular, has proven to be a potent instrument for awareness and mobilization, enabling activists to connect with a global audience and galvanize international support.

The challenges faced by grassroots activists are manifold, including limited resources, burnout, and, at times, confrontations with powerful adversaries. Yet, it is their resilience and adaptability that allows them to navigate these obstacles, driven by an unwavering commitment to justice and human rights.

In the fight against human trafficking, the role of faith cannot be underestimated. Many grassroots organizations draw upon spiritual principles to sustain their efforts, finding strength and guidance in their convictions. This spiritual dimension enriches the activism, imbuing it with a sense of purpose that transcends the material and the immediate.

The essence of grassroots activism lies in its ability to empower individuals, harnessing the collective power of communities in pursuit of a world free from exploitation. It's a reminder that each of us holds the potential to effect change, to light a candle in the darkness. As we stand together, our joined forces can turn the tide against human trafficking, paving the way towards liberation and healing.

In conclusion, the fight against human trafficking is a battle waged on many fronts. Among these, grassroots activism stands out for its impact, resilience, and capacity to engage the heart of communities. It embodies the belief that change is within our grasp, that together, we can forge a future where freedom and dignity prevail for all.

Supporting Victims in Your Community

In addressing the profound scourge of human trafficking, it becomes imperative to not only confront the perpetrators but also to extend a hand of solace and assistance to the victims ensnared by this heinous crime. Within our communities lie the untapped potential and the moral obligation to be sanctuaries of healing and hope for those who have been subjected to such grievous injustices.

At the heart of community efforts to support victims is the principle of empathy, a virtue deeply rooted in the teachings and example of Christ Himself. It is through empathy that we can begin to understand the profound trauma experienced by victims of trafficking and, thus, tailor our assistance to meet their multifaceted needs (Plant, 2013).

One of the initial steps towards supporting victims in your community is to cultivate a culture of awareness and understanding. Misconceptions and lack of knowledge about human trafficking can often hinder efforts to assist victims effectively. Education campaigns, seminars, and workshops can illuminate the realities of trafficking, dismantle myths, and prepare community members to identify and assist victims properly.

Fostering partnerships between community organizations, law enforcement, and faith-based groups is crucial. These collaborations ensure that efforts are coordinated, and resources are pooled to provide comprehensive support to victims. Such alliances can create safe havens where victims can find shelter, legal assistance, counseling, and spiritual care.

Offering specialized support services is another critical aspect of aiding trafficking survivors. Securing access to trauma-informed healthcare, legal representation to navigate immigration or criminal justice issues, and employment training programs can drastically impact a survivor's journey toward rebuilding their lives.

Advocacy plays a pivotal role in supporting victims at the community level. Efforts to influence local policies, push for the allocation of resources towards victim services, and raise public consciousness about trafficking can foster an environment that prioritizes the needs and rights of victims.

Spiritual care, often overlooked, is vital in addressing the deep wounds trafficking inflicts on its victims. Offering spaces for spiritual healing, guided by the principles of compassion, forgiveness, and redemption, can aid in the holistic recovery of survivors.

Volunteerism is the backbone of community efforts in supporting trafficking survivors. Volunteers can offer their time, skills, and resources in various capacities - from staffing hotlines to providing mentorship or tutoring services to survivors attempting to rebuild their lives.

In this noble endeavor, it's paramount that efforts to support victims are guided by respect for their dignity and autonomy. A survivor-centered approach that respects the wishes, privacy, and safety of victims ensures that assistance provided truly benefits them without inadvertently causing further harm.

Creating awareness and training programs for professionals who might come into contact with victims, such as healthcare workers, educators, and law enforcement personnel, can lead to early identification and intervention, significantly affecting outcomes for trafficking survivors.

Community-based initiatives, such as safe house programs and survivor advocacy groups, can empower victims through peer support and shared experiences. These initiatives not only aid in recovery but also inculcate a sense of belonging and purpose among survivors.

In leveraging technology, communities can offer innovative solutions to support victims. From developing apps that provide resources and information to victims discreetly, to using social media platforms to spread awareness and advocate for policy changes, the digital realm holds immense potential for amplifying efforts to aid trafficking survivors (Aderemi and Adewole, 2022).

Lastly, institutions of learning, by integrating education on human trafficking into their curriculums, can nurture a forthcoming generation that is not only well-informed about the issue but also passionate about contributing to the eradication of trafficking and supporting victims in tangible ways.

Every individual possesses the ability to contribute to the healing and empowerment of trafficking victims. It is through our collective action, grounded in empathy, compassion, and a commitment to justice, that we can hope to mend the fabric of our communities, torn asunder by the evils of trafficking. Let us, therefore, respond to this call with unwavering resolve, harnessing our resources, skills, and faith to forge pathways of recovery and resilience for those who have suffered too much, for too long.

Chapter 13: Economic Factors and Solutions

In the exploration of the intricate labyrinth that is human trafficking, economic forces emerge as both the fuel for its perpetuation and the keys to its dissolution. At the heart of this conundrum lies the demand for trafficked labor and services, a dark mirror reflecting our society's highest and lowest values. Recognizing this, strategies for economic empowerment become not just interventions but moral imperatives for those seeking justice. By forging paths toward financial independence and stability for at-risk populations, we illuminate the way out of exploitation. Initiatives encouraging fair trade and ethical consumption cut the financial lifelines of exploitative industries, revealing the strength of the market as a force for good when wielded with conscience (Broderick, 2005). Moreover, investment in education and vocational training equips those vulnerable to trafficking with the armor of self-sufficiency, challenging the economic desperation that traffickers exploit (Punam and Sharma, 2018). This dual approach, attacking both supply and demand, creates a sustainable framework for dismantling trafficking networks. However, as we refine these solutions, we must also remain vigilant, understanding that economic landscapes are ever-changing, and so too must our strategies adapt (Bales, 2020). Thus, as we navigate through the tumultuous waters of economic factors, we anchor our efforts in the pursuit of dignity for all, mindful that in the battle against human trafficking, our most potent weapon is our shared humanity.

The Demand for Trafficked Labor and Services

In the quest to comprehensively address human trafficking, a significant area necessitates thorough exploration-the demand for trafficked labor and services. This demand, both insidious and widespread, fuels the underground market, perpetuating a cycle of exploitation and suffering. An analysis of this demand, its roots, and its sustenance is critical to formulating viable solutions.

At the heart of the demand for trafficked labor and services lies a stark economic reality: the pursuit of reduced costs and maximized profits. Industries across various sectors, from agriculture to construction, from domestic work to the sex trade, often seek the cheapest labor possible to maintain or increase profit margins. This quest frequently leads to the exploitation of vulnerable populations, where traffickers fill the demand with forced or coerced labor.

The nature of consumerism itself, with its relentless demand for lower prices and an ever-available supply of goods and services, inadvertently encourages the proliferation of trafficking networks. Most consumers remain unaware of the real human cost embedded in the products and services they enjoy. This disconnects between consumption and its consequences plays a crucial role in sustaining trafficking operations (Blanton and Blanton, 2020).

Government policies and law enforcement practices also impact the demand for trafficked labor. Laws that inadequately protect worker rights or fail to penalize companies benefiting from exploitative labor practices indirectly boost the profitability of trafficking. The lack of stringent enforcement of existing labor laws creates an environment where trafficked labor can thrive under the guise of legitimate employment.

Societal attitudes towards migration and labor significantly influence the demand for trafficked labor. In many cases, prejudices and stereotypes marginalize certain groups, rendering them more vulnerable to exploitation. Migrants seeking better opportunities, for instance, often find themselves ensnared in trafficking networks that promise employment but deliver enslavement.

The exploitation of individuals through trafficking for labor and services is fundamentally a violation of their dignity. From a standpoint of faith, every human being is endowed with inherent dignity and rights, a view underscored by numerous theological and ethical frameworks. Recognizing the sacredness of each person is paramount in confronting and challenging the demand for trafficked labor.

Education plays a pivotal role in diminishing the demand for trafficked labor and services. Awareness campaigns aimed at both consumers and corporations can illuminate the human costs behind products and services. Informed consumers can exert significant pressure on companies to ensure ethical practices along their supply chains, thus reducing the reliance on trafficked labor.

Furthermore, enhancing legal frameworks to protect workers and punish those who exploit trafficked labor is essential. Strengthening labor rights, increasing transparency in business operations, and enforcing strict penalties for violations can diminish the profitability of trafficking operations. Such measures would serve not only as deterrents but also as affirmations of societal commitment to justice and human rights.

A holistic approach towards eradicating the demand for trafficked labor must also entail economic empowerment for vulnerable populations. By providing access to education, vocational training, and fair employment opportunities, communities can shield their members from the vulnerabilities trafficker's exploit. Economic empowerment serves both as a preventative measure and as a pathway to recovery for those who have survived trafficking (Broderick, 2005).

Intersectoral cooperation is vital in tackling the demand for trafficked labor. Governments, non-profit organizations, faith-based groups, businesses, and consumers must collaborate to address this multifaceted issue. Each sector brings unique resources and perspectives that can contribute to a comprehensive solution.

Consumer advocacy for ethical consumption practices can significantly impact the demand for trafficked labor. By choosing products and services verified as free from exploitation, consumers can drive the market towards more ethical practices. Such choices, while seemingly small, aggregate to a powerful force for change.

On a broader scale, international cooperation is crucial in combating human trafficking. Trafficking networks often operate across borders, exploiting differences in legal standards and enforcement practices. Enhanced international collaboration, including shared legal standards and coordinated enforcement actions, can close the gaps trafficked labor slips through.

The demand for trafficked labor is not an insurmountable issue. With concerted efforts grounded in a deep understanding of its economic, social, and moral dimensions, significant progress can be made towards its eradication. It calls for a moral awakening that recognizes the dignity and worth of every individual and commits to protecting those virtues through concrete action.

As communities of faith, scholars, policymakers, and citizens unite in this cause, the darkness that is human trafficking can be confronted with the light of justice, truth, and love. Let this endeavor be rooted not only in the desire to end suffering but in the commitment to uphold the dignity of every person, reflecting the profound respect for human life that underpins our society.

In conclusion, the demand for trafficked labor and services, while daunting, is not invincible. Addressing it requires a multifaceted strategy that combines economic, legal, educational, and moral approaches. It is a challenge that demands the best of our humanity—our compassion, our diligence, and our unwavering commitment to justice. Together, through collective action and a steadfast belief in the dignity of all, we can forge a future free from the scourge of trafficking.

Strategies for Economic Empowerment

Within the complex network of factors contributing to the scourge of human trafficking, the economic dimension holds a central position. It's an undeniable truth that financial instability can significantly heighten the vulnerability of individuals to exploitation. Therefore, strategies aimed at economic empowerment emerge not merely as beneficial, but as essential in the fight against this egregious violation of human dignity.

The scriptures remind us of the importance of aiding the poor and the oppressed, situating economic empowerment as a moral imperative. It is not enough to rescue and rehabilitate; there must be sustainable opportunities for those at risk, preventing them from falling prey to traffickers. This approach entails a multifaceted strategy incorporating education, skill development, and access to fair employment opportunities (Cordisco Tsai, 2022).

Education is the cornerstone of economic empowerment. Illuminating minds not only paves the way for personal development but also equips individuals with the knowledge to discern exploitative situations. A well-informed person is less likely to be ensnared by the false promises of traffickers. Thus, increasing access to quality education, especially for marginalized communities, is paramount.

Moreover, skill development programs tailored to the needs of the labor market can significantly enhance employability and income potential. These programs should aim to bridge the gap between the skills possessed by the individual and those demanded by employers. Vocational training, apprenticeships, and technical education are vital components of this strategy.

Access to fair employment opportunities is equally critical. Efforts to stimulate job creation in underdeveloped regions can help mitigate one of the key economic drivers of trafficking. This requires collaboration between governments, businesses, and non-profit organizations to foster an environment conducive to economic growth and the creation of decent work for all.

Microfinancing initiatives also hold promise as tools for economic empowerment. By providing small loans to those unable to access traditional banking services, these programs enable individuals to start their own businesses. This, in turn, can lead to increased economic independence and a reduction in vulnerability to human trafficking. It's a testament to the principle that empowerment through economic means can serve as a potent weapon in our arsenal against trafficking.

Furthermore, promoting fair trade practices can contribute to economic empowerment by ensuring that workers in supply chains receive a fair wage and work under humane conditions.

Consumers have a powerful role in this regard; by choosing to support companies that adhere to ethical practices, they can help diminish the demand for trafficked labor.

Engaging the private sector is indispensable in these efforts. Businesses must be encouraged to implement policies that prevent human trafficking in their supply chains. This includes conducting thorough audits, offering training to employees on identifying and responding to signs of trafficking, and establishing transparent reporting mechanisms.

At the legislative level, policies aimed at reducing poverty and inequality can lay the groundwork for economic empowerment. Social protection schemes, access to healthcare, and affordable housing can alleviate some of the economic pressures that leave individuals vulnerable to trafficking.

Investment in communities as a whole is necessary to address systemic issues contributing to trafficking. Infrastructure projects, such as improving transportation and access to technology, can have wide-ranging benefits, including opening up new economic opportunities.

The role of faith-based organizations in economic empowerment cannot be overlooked. With their extensive networks and commitment to social justice, these organizations are uniquely positioned to provide support and resources to those in need.

Initiatives like job training, education programs, and social enterprises can significantly impact individuals' lives.

Ultimately, economic empowerment strategies must be inclusive and adaptive. They should be designed with a deep understanding of the specific needs and conditions of the target communities. This ensures that interventions are not only effective but also respectful of the dignity and autonomy of the individuals they aim to serve (Barrows, 2017).

In conclusion, the pursuit of economic empowerment as a strategy against human trafficking is both a pragmatic and a moral imperative. It aligns with the values we hold dear and offers a tangible path towards a future where everyone has the opportunity to live free from exploitation. As we join hands in this endeavor, let us be guided by wisdom, compassion, and an unwavering commitment to justice.

"For I, the Lord, love justice; I hate robbery and wrongdoing. In my faithfulness, I will reward my people and make an everlasting covenant with them." - Isaiah 61:8

Chapter 14: Survivor Stories: Lessons of Hope and Resilience

As we delve into the heartrending yet ultimately inspiring accounts of those who have endured and triumphed over the evils of human trafficking, it becomes evident that each story is a testament to the indomitable spirit of hope and resilience. The journey from victim to survivor to advocate is fraught with unimaginable challenges, yet it is precisely this journey that illuminates the potential for profound transformation and healing. Survivors' narratives not only offer a glimpse into the darkest corners of human exploitation but also shine a light on the remarkable strength and courage inherent in the human spirit. Through their experiences, survivors provide invaluable lessons on the power of perseverance, the importance of community support, and the transformative potential of faith and forgiveness in the healing process.

The path to recovery and empowerment for survivors is both complex and deeply personal. It often involves navigating the intricacies of the legal system, rebuilding trust with oneself and others, and finding ways to heal from the physical and psychological scars left by their experiences. Organizations such as the Polaris Project and Shared Hope International have been instrumental in providing the support and resources necessary for survivors to reclaim their lives and identities (Hutchinson,

2021). Moreover, faith-based initiatives offer a unique form of solace and strength, underscoring the role of spiritual healing in overcoming trauma. The stories of survivors who have found refuge and renewal through their faith reveal the profound impact of spiritual resilience in the face of adversity (Aliotta, 2021).

In sharing their stories, survivors perform an invaluable service to society, educating the public about the realities of human trafficking while advocating for change. Their firsthand accounts serve as a powerful call to action, urging individuals, communities, and policymakers to join the fight against trafficking. By listening to and learning from these survivor stories, we are reminded of the critical importance of compassion, understanding, and collective action in addressing this global scourge. As we reflect on these lessons of hope and resilience, we are inspired to renew our commitment to ending human trafficking and supporting those who have been most deeply affected by it (Viergever et al., 2018).

Chapter 15: Prevention and Education Programs

In the crusade against the malevolent tide of human trafficking that sweeps across our nation, prevention and education emerge not merely as shields, but as formidable weapons capable of altering the very landscape of this battle. Within the educational sphere, there is a paramount need to incorporate comprehensive programs that not merely inform but empower our youth with the discernment and strength to resist the snares of traffickers. School-based initiatives, as highlighted in recent studies, have shown a marked efficacy in not only raising awareness among students but also in fostering an environment where children feel equipped to navigate the complexities of interactions both in the real world and online (Greenbaum et al., 2018). The curriculum designed for these programs does not shy away from the harsh realities, but rather, approaches them with a delicate balance of truth and hope, ensuring that while students are made aware of the dangers, they are also instilled with the wisdom to act and protect themselves and their peers.

Beyond the confines of educational institutions, community awareness campaigns serve as a beacon of light, reaching out to the corners of society often overshadowed by ignorance or indifference. These campaigns, deeply rooted in the principles of empathy and solidarity, strive to weave a narrative that human trafficking is not a distant problem but a pervasive blight affecting communities on a micro level. By partnering with local businesses, faith-based organizations, and law enforcement, these campaigns dismantle the myths surrounding trafficking, presenting facts and stories that resonate deeply within the collective consciousness of the community (Diaz et al., 2021). It is through these concerted efforts that a once-muted topic becomes a clarion call to action, galvanizing communities to stand united against this scourge.

The synergy of school-based initiatives and community awareness campaigns lays the groundwork for a society that refuses to turn a blind eye to the specter of human trafficking. Yet, the success of these programs hinges upon continuous support, research, and adaptation to confront the ever-evolving tactics of traffickers. As we marshal forward, it is imperative that these prevention and education programs are embraced not as optional undertakings but as indispensable components of a holistic strategy to eradicate human trafficking from the fabric of our nation. In this unified quest, let it be known that our resolve is unwavering, our efforts tireless, and our spirits indomitable, for in the words of the wise, the battle for dignity and freedom is fought not just on the fields of justice, but in the hearts and minds of every individual willing to heed the call.

School-Based Initiatives

In the multifaceted struggle against the blight of human trafficking, the arena of education stands poised as a bastion of prevention and awareness. Within the sacred halls of learning, there exists an unparalleled opportunity to arm the young minds with knowledge, and henceforth, power. The essence of school-based initiatives in combating human trafficking lies not only in the dissemination of knowledge but in fostering a generation of vigilant and empowered individuals.

At the core of these initiatives is the curriculum integration focused on human trafficking. This involves developing and incorporating comprehensive educational materials designed to enlighten students on the realities of trafficking. By integrating discussions concerning the forms, signs, and consequences of human trafficking into the curriculum, educators can cultivate an informed student body. The purpose is not to instill fear, but to empower students with the knowledge to protect themselves and their peers (Zhu et al., 2020).

Training educators and school administrators plays a pivotal role in the effectiveness of school-based initiatives. It's not merely about imparting knowledge but equipping these trusted figures with the ability to recognize potential signs of trafficking among their students. Furthermore, they're trained on how to respond to disclosures sensitively and effectively, creating a safe environment for students to report concerns.

Peer education programs emerge as a potent tool within schools. These programs empower students to be the harbingers of awareness among their peers, fostering a culture of vigilance and mutual care. When students are taught by their contemporaries, the message of prevention and awareness is often received more openly, cultivating a school environment where students look out for one another.

School partnerships with local law enforcement and organizations fighting against human trafficking fortify these initiatives. These partnerships not only facilitate expert-led workshops and seminars but also ensure that students have access to authentic information and real-world examples of trafficking scenarios and successful interventions.

Creating safe spaces within schools for discussion and inquiry about human trafficking is vital. Such spaces encourage students to voice concerns, ask questions, and explore solutions in a supportive environment. It's about nurturing a culture where the taboo surrounding discussions of exploitation is dismantled (Pooler et al., 2022).

Engaging parents and guardians in these initiatives is equally crucial. Workshops and informational sessions that involve the student's family can extend the dialogue beyond school premises, ensuring that awareness and vigilance become a community-wide effort.

Art and media projects related to human trafficking can be an expressive outlet for students, helping to raise awareness in creative ways. These projects not only foster empathy and understanding but also enable students to advocate against trafficking through their art, reaching wider audiences.

Critical thinking and ethical reasoning related to human trafficking should be nurtured in students. This involves encouraging them to think deeply about the broader societal and ethical issues surrounding trafficking, fostering a generation of critical thinkers and ethical leaders.

Schools should also provide opportunities for students to engage in activism and advocacy. This could involve organizing awareness events, participating in community outreach programs, and advocating for policy changes at local, state, and national levels. Such activities empower students, giving them a sense of agency in the fight against human trafficking.

Monitoring and evaluation of these school-based initiatives are paramount to ensure their effectiveness and sustainability. It is essential to collect data and feedback to understand the impact of these programs on students' knowledge, attitudes, and behaviors regarding human trafficking.

It is crucial to remember, however, that these educational efforts must be age-appropriate. Discussions and content should be tailored to suit the cognitive and emotional maturity of the students, ensuring that the message is conveyed effectively without causing undue distress (Diaz et al., 2021).

The challenge of human trafficking in our society calls for a multidimensional approach, wherein the role of education is indispensable. School-based initiatives offer a beacon of hope, illuminating the path toward a world where the chains of exploitation are broken, and freedom reigns. It's an endeavor that requires the collective effort of educators, students, parents, and the wider community. Together, we can forge a future where human trafficking finds no refuge.

Community Awareness Campaigns

Within the encompassing journey towards the eradication of human trafficking, community awareness campaigns emerge as a beacon of hope and action. These campaigns serve not only as an educational tool but also as a rallying cry for communities to unify against this plague that undermines human dignity and freedom. Envisioned and executed with precision, these campaigns possess the singular ability to alter perceptions, inform the uninformed, and galvanize communities into tangible action against human trafficking.

The genesis of effective community awareness campaigns lies in understanding the nuanced nature of human trafficking. Armed with knowledge, organizers can tailor their messages to highlight the pervasive yet often hidden presence of trafficking within local contexts. It is a task that requires astuteness, for the signs of human trafficking are frequently masked behind the façade of normalcy, eluding the untrained eye (Aderemi and Adewole, 2022).

Central to the philosophy of these campaigns is the concept of informed empathy. It's not enough to merely inform; one must connect on a human level, fostering a deep sense of empathy and urgency. Effective campaigns thus weave narratives that are both compelling and relatable, bridging the gap between abstract statistics and the real human suffering they represent. This narrative approach mirrors the parabolic teachings that have long been used to impart moral lessons through relatable storytelling.

Fostering partnerships is another cornerstone of impactful community awareness campaigns. By collaborating with local schools, churches, law enforcement, and businesses, organizers can create a multifaceted approach that penetrates various spheres of community life. Each sector brings unique resources and perspectives, enriching the campaign and extending its reach.

Digital platforms have radically transformed the landscape of community awareness campaigns. Social media, in particular, has proven to be a powerful tool for amplifying messages, reaching out to younger demographics, and facilitating discussions around topics that were once confined to more formal or controlled settings. Tailored content that is both engaging and educational can virally spread awareness, making it a critical component of contemporary campaigns.

However, despite the advances in digital communication, the importance of grassroots, face-to-face interactions cannot be overstated. Community events, workshops, and seminars provide invaluable opportunities for deep engagement. These interactions allow for the dissemination of knowledge in ways that are personal and impactful, often leaving a lasting impression on participants.

Measurement and evaluation are imperative to evolving and strengthening community awareness campaigns. By setting clear objectives and employing both qualitative and quantitative metrics, organizers can gain insights into the effectiveness of their efforts. Feedback loops enable the refinement of strategies, ensuring that campaigns remain relevant and impactful (Mobasher et al., 2022).

The ethical component of community awareness campaigns cannot be neglected. Sensitivity to victims' experiences and a commitment to truthful representation are paramount. The dignity of survivors must be preserved at all costs, with their stories shared in a manner that is respectful and consensual.

Within the tapestry of these campaigns, stories of hope and resilience emerge as powerful motifs. Survivor stories, when shared with respect and care, can significantly alter public perception and understanding of human trafficking. These narratives, rich with personal triumph over adversity, serve as a testament to the human spirit's indomitability.

Engaging the youth in community awareness campaigns introduces freshness and dynamism. Young people bring innovative ideas and are adept at leveraging new technologies for social change. Through school clubs, youth groups, and social media, they can become fervent advocates for the cause, influencing their peers and families.

Religious communities hold a unique place in the context of community awareness campaigns. Their foundational commitments to justice and care for the marginalized make them natural allies in the fight against human trafficking. Through sermons, community gatherings, and social justice ministries, they can amplify the message, grounded in a deep moral and ethical conviction.

Law enforcement agencies play a dual role in these campaigns: as sources of vital information and as active participants. Their insights into the mechanisms of trafficking and tales of rescue operations provide compelling content for awareness efforts. Furthermore, their involvement lends credibility and seriousness to the issue, highlighting the legal implications and the committed fight against traffickers.

The call to political activism is a recurring theme in community awareness campaigns. By educating the public about the significance of legislation and the power of their vote, campaigns can mobilize communities to advocate for stronger laws and policies against human trafficking. This approach fosters a sense of collective responsibility and empowerment.

Finally, community awareness campaigns must be seen as an ongoing journey rather than a destination. As societies evolve and new challenges emerge, these campaigns must adapt, innovate, and persist. The fight against human trafficking is a testament to humanity's resilience, compassion, and unwavering commitment to freedom and dignity for all.

In conclusion, community awareness campaigns stand out as critical components in the multi-faceted approach to combating human trafficking. Through education, empathy, and Engaging various community stakeholders, these campaigns contribute significantly to shedding light on a dark issue. By emphasizing human dignity and leveraging collective action, we move step by step closer to a world free of human trafficking (Zhu et al., 2020).

Chapter 16: Health Care Professionals' Role

In the multifaceted battle against human trafficking, health care professionals hold a unique position of influence and responsibility. Often, these individuals are on the frontlines, potentially interacting with victims during their exploitation phase. Given this critical intersection, it's imperative that the medical community is equipped with the knowledge and tools necessary to recognize the signs of trafficking and to respond effectively. Training for health care providers, therefore, becomes a cornerstone in the fight against this egregious violation of human rights. It's not merely about identifying victims based on physical signs of abuse; there's a deeper, more complex layer involving psychological trauma that must be navigated with compassion and understanding. Furthermore, the role of healthcare professionals isn't confined to identification and immediate care. There's a broader aspect of assisting in the recovery and rehabilitation process, offering a bridge from the despair of trafficking to the hope of freedom and healing. This chapter delves into the critical aspects of recognizing signs of human trafficking within health care settings, outlines the best practices for training health care providers, and emphasizes the long-term role of medical professionals in the journey of recovery for trafficking survivors (Ahn et al., 2013). Through a comprehensive approach that marries the acuity of medical knowledge with the sensitivities required to care for traumatized individuals, health care professionals can significantly contribute to the dismantling of human trafficking networks and the restoration of dignity and health to its victims.

Identifying and Assisting Victims

In the continuing battle against human trafficking, health care professionals hold a uniquely pivotal role. Their frontline position in society not only enables them to identify victims of trafficking but also to offer crucial first steps towards rehabilitation. It's an undertaking that calls for vigilance, compassion, and an understanding of the subtleties that distinguish the physical and psychological markers of trafficking.

First and foremost, the ability to recognize the signs of human trafficking within a clinical setting is fundamental. Victims may present with a range of indicators, from physical injuries consistent with abuse to more nuanced signs such as a lack of control over personal identification documents (Hopper & Hidalgo, 2021). Health care professionals must be attuned to these cues, understanding that they may represent a piece in the larger puzzle of a patient's predicament.

Moreover, creating a safe space for potential victims to disclose their situations is central to the identification process. The approach, tone, and environment can significantly impact a victim's willingness to communicate, requiring staff to foster a sense of trust and confidentiality. It's about striking a delicate balance; being direct yet gentle, authoritative yet empathetic (Grace et al., 2014).

Once suspicion arises, it's imperative that health care providers have a clear and ethical protocol to follow. This involves knowing whom to contact within the legal and social services networks without escalating the risk to the victim's safety. The reporting process should be discreet, aimed at initiating the victim's journey towards liberation and recovery while safeguarding them from further harm.

Assisting victims further entails a multidisciplinary approach, calling upon the expertise of social workers, legal professionals, and mental health counselors. It's an ecosystem of support, designed to provide holistic care that addresses the physical, psychological, and legal needs of the victim. Health care professionals must act as the linchpin in this network, coordinating care and ensuring the victim's comprehensive needs are met.

Educational programs targeted at health care workers are crucial in equipping them with the tools necessary to identify and assist victims effectively. Training should cover a wide range of topics, from the socio-economic drivers of trafficking to the psychological impact on victims. Knowledge, after all, empowers action.

Furthermore, the ethical implications of treating trafficking victims cannot be overstated. Health care professionals must navigate the delicate balance between patient confidentiality and the moral imperative to intervene. This ethical quandary requires a deep understanding of professional responsibilities and the legal frameworks governing patient care and reportage (Chisolm-Straker et al., 2019).

In addition to recognizing and reporting, there's an imperative to address the aftermath of trafficking. Victims often grapple with a host of health issues—from physical traumas to complex psychological disorders such as PTSD. Tailoring health interventions to meet these varied needs is essential, underscoring the importance of specialized training for health care professionals in dealing with post-trafficking care.

Prevention also falls within the purview of health care's role against trafficking. By identifying and addressing risk factors in patients—such as substance abuse or precarious living situations-professionals can play a proactive role in preventing exploitation before it occurs. It's about being attentive to the vulnerabilities in patients that traffickers may exploit.

Moreover, partnerships between health care institutions and anti-trafficking organizations can amplify efforts to combat trafficking. These collaborations can facilitate the sharing of information, resources, and best practices. They serve not only to enhance the identification and care of victims but also to foster a broader culture of awareness and prevention within communities.

It's also crucial for health care providers to understand the diversity among trafficking victims. Trafficking does not discriminate by age, gender, or ethnicity, and as such, professionals must be equipped to recognize and assist a wide array of individuals. Sensitivity to cultural, gender, and age-specific issues is paramount, requiring ongoing education and self-reflection.

Legal advocacy is another area where health care professionals can contribute significantly. By providing medical documentation of abuse and exploitation, they can support victims' legal cases, facilitating their quest for justice and restitution. This aspect of care underscores the intersection between health care and the legal battle against trafficking.

The emotional toll on health care professionals involved in this work should not be underestimated. Dealing with the gross injustices of trafficking can lead to burnout and secondary traumatic stress. Institutions must ensure that support systems are in place for staff, promoting resilience and self-care to sustain their crucial efforts in this challenging field.

In conclusion, the role of health care professionals in identifying and assisting victims of human trafficking is both vital and multifaceted. It requires a blend of clinical acumen, ethical discernment, and compassionate care. As they stand at the intersection of health and justice, their contribution is not merely professional; it's profoundly humanitarian, anchored in the fundamental right to freedom and dignity for all individuals.

Ultimately, it's through informed, sustained, and collaborative efforts that health care providers can make a tangible difference in the lives of trafficking victims, offering not just medical relief, but a pathway to healing and liberation. This dignified endeavor not only resonates with the ethical imperatives of the medical profession but also with the moral convictions that underpin our society, urging us onwards in the fight against trafficking.

Training for Health Care Providers

As we delve deeper into the crucial role of health care professionals in the fight against human trafficking, it becomes apparent that specialized training is not just beneficial but essential. Within the confines of this battle, knowledge is power, and for health care providers, it's the power to change lives. The intersection of health care and human trafficking presents a unique opportunity for intervention, making it imperative that those on the medical front lines are well-prepared to act.

It's no secret that victims of trafficking may come into contact with health care systems at various points during their exploitation. These encounters provide a critical window for identification and intervention. However, without the proper training, signs of trafficking can easily be missed or misinterpreted. It's akin to looking for a needle in a haystack without knowing what a needle looks like. Thus, training programs specifically designed for health care providers are not just necessary; they are a moral imperative (Dovydaitis, 2010).

The essence of such training revolves around several key components. First and foremost is the ability to recognize the signs and symptoms of trafficking. This includes understanding the physical and psychological indicators, as well as the less obvious signs that might present in a clinical setting. Trafficking victims often come with a complex set of health issues, ranging from physical injuries to psychological trauma. A trained eye can discern the subtle cues that hint at a deeper story of coercion or abuse.

Another critical aspect of training involves learning how to approach a suspected victim of trafficking. The principles of compassion, empathy, and non-judgment must underpin every interaction. Patients who are victims of trafficking often experience a profound sense of shame and distrust. As such, the manner in which health care providers engage with them can either open the door to intervention or further entrench their isolation.

Confidentiality and safety are paramount in these situations. Training must cover the protocols for protecting patient information, as well as understanding the legal and ethical obligations involved in reporting trafficking. Navigating these waters can be incredibly complex, requiring a delicate balance between acting and respecting the autonomy and wishes of the patient.

Beyond identification and initial engagement, health care providers also need training in providing care that is sensitive to the trauma experienced by trafficking victims. Trauma-informed care recognizes the widespread impact of trauma and understands potential paths for recovery. It seeks to avoid re-traumatization and places a strong emphasis on safety, choice, and control for the patient.

Moreover, training should also include an overview of the resources and services available for trafficking victims. Health care providers should be familiar with the network of support available, from specialized trafficking intervention programs to local social services. Being able to provide victims with information about these resources is an essential step in supporting their journey out of trafficking.

Finally, continuous education and training updates are vital. The landscape of human trafficking is ever-evolving, as are the tools and methods for intervention. Ongoing training ensures that health care providers remain at the forefront of best practices in identifying and assisting victims of trafficking.

Implementing such comprehensive training programs requires collaboration across multiple sectors, including health care institutions, trafficking experts, and survivor advocates. It's a multifaceted effort that demands time, resources, and a commitment to change. However, the potential impact of well-trained health care professionals in the fight against trafficking cannot be overstated.

In conclusion, equipping health care providers with the knowledge and skills to recognize and respond to human trafficking is a vital component of a broader strategy to combat this form of modern-day slavery. The call to action is clear: training for health care providers is not just an option; it's an ethical obligation. Through education, awareness, and compassion, health care professionals can play a pivotal role in breaking the chains of trafficking, one life at a time.

Chapter 17: Media Representation and Responsibility

In the endeavor to obliterate the scourge of human trafficking from our midst, the media wields a double-edged sword; it has the capacity to both illuminate the darkest corners where injustice breeds and inadvertently perpetuate harmful stereotypes or oversimplify complex narratives. Ethical reporting on trafficking demands a meticulous approach, one that respects victims' dignity without compromising the stark reality of their plight (Dryhurst, 2012). The media's portrayal of human trafficking is pivotal, shaping public perception and influencing policy decisions. The responsible dissemination of information calls for a commitment to accuracy, a rejection of sensationalism, and an empathetic lens towards those affected (Brown, 2010). Furthermore, harnessing the power of media in advocacy ushers a beacon of hope; well-crafted narratives and informed reporting can mobilize society, inspiring actions that range from legislative changes to grassroots movements (O'Brien, 2016).

Ethical Reporting on Trafficking

In the mission to combat human trafficking, the media serves as a powerful tool, shaping public perception and influencing policy decisions. However, this power comes with substantial responsibility. Ethical reporting on trafficking is paramount to ensure that the narrative being shared respects the dignity of survivors, educates the public, and supports the broader fight against this pervasive injustice.

The essence of ethical journalism lies in its commitment to truth, accuracy, and fairness. When covering stories on human trafficking, reporters must navigate the complexities of these cases with sensitivity and integrity. The specter of sensationalism looms large, and the temptation to prioritize a compelling narrative over the wellbeing of survivors can present a moral quandary.

Human trafficking, in its nefarious forms, challenges our societal fabric, exploiting the vulnerable and marginalized. The media's portrayal of trafficking scenarios can sometimes inadvertently perpetuate stereotypes or stigmatize survivors, a consequence that ethical journalism strives to avoid. It is incumbent upon reporters to craft their stories with a deep understanding of the human rights issues at play, recognizing the survivors' courage and resilience (Downman et al., 2017).

Confidentiality and privacy are sacrosanct principles in reporting on human trafficking. Survivors' identities must be protected unless they have given informed consent, understanding fully how their stories will be shared. The trauma of trafficking can be re-experienced through public exposure, making it imperative for journalists to proceed with caution and empathy.

The portrayal of trafficking in the media can also influence law enforcement and policy measures. Accurate, informed reporting can spur action and advocacy, shining a light on gaps in the legal framework or enforcement efforts. It is, therefore, vital for journalists to conduct thorough research, consulting with experts and utilizing reputable sources to ground their reporting in fact.

Language plays a critical role in ethical journalism. Terms that might dehumanize or blame the victims of trafficking should be meticulously avoided. Instead, the lexicon used must reflect the dignity of each individual and the gravity of their experiences. This care with words extends to depicting trafficking not as a choice someone makes, but as a violation of their freedom and rights (Curtis, 2012).

Moreover, the media has the capacity to educate the public on recognizing the signs of human trafficking and understanding its root causes. Through ethical reporting, journalists can demystify misconceptions, providing a clear-eyed view of the scale and complexity of trafficking. Such reporting empowers communities, equipping them with knowledge to potentially identify and prevent trafficking situations.

Yet, the responsibility of the media does not end with publication. The ongoing monitoring of the impact of stories about trafficking is crucial. Feedback should be sought, particularly from survivors and those working on the frontlines. This reflective practice ensures that reporting evolves and continues to uphold the highest ethical standards.

The ethical challenges in reporting on human trafficking are manifold, necessitating a deliberate and considered approach. Journalists must balance the public's right to know with the potential harm that reporting can inflict on survivors. This balancing act requires not only adherence to journalistic principles but also a moral compass guided by compassion and respect for human dignity.

Engagement with survivors and advocacy groups can enhance the quality and sensitivity of reporting. These interactions offer insights into the personal and systemic dimensions of trafficking, enriching the narrative and ensuring that it serves the interests of justice and awareness. However, this engagement must be conducted with the utmost respect for the autonomy and desires of survivors.

Education and training for journalists on the complexities of human trafficking are indispensable. This specialized knowledge enables reporters to approach their work with the nuance and depth it demands. Media organizations have a role to play in providing such training and fostering an environment where ethical considerations are at the forefront of trafficking coverage.

Ultimately, ethical reporting on trafficking contributes to a more informed and compassionate society. It can challenge preconceptions, highlight the need for change, and inspire action. In fulfilling this role, the media not only reports on trafficking but actively participates in the global effort to eradicate it.

In conclusion, ethical reporting on human trafficking is a critical aspect of media responsibility. It requires a careful balance of truth-telling and sensitivity, respect for survivors, and a commitment to human rights. As the media continues to navigate this challenging terrain, it must remain vigilant in its ethics, compassionate in its storytelling, and unwavering in its pursuit of justice.

The Power of Media in Advocacy

In the contemporary epoch, the influence wielded by the media is both profound and far-reaching. Media, in its multifaceted forms, plays a pivotal role in shaping public opinion and, more importantly, in advocating for social change. This section delves into the profound capacity of media to mold perceptions, inform the masses, and galvanize collective action against the heinous crime of human trafficking. It endeavors to unravel the symbiotic relationship between media and advocacy, underscoring how strategic communication can illuminate the dark recesses where injustice flourishes (Jedlowski, 2018).

Human trafficking, a complex and clandestine operation, thrives in shadows, away from the scrutiny of the public eye. However, the media, with its penetrating gaze, can cast light upon these obscured narratives, granting them the visibility necessary for societal intervention. The authority of the media to unveil the truth cannot be underestimated; it serves as a beacon, guiding the collective conscience towards issues otherwise shrouded in apathy.

The role of media in advocacy transcends mere reportage; it embodies the capacity to evoke empathy, induce outrage, and inspire action. Through compelling storytelling, the media can humanize the statistical realities of trafficking, transforming abstract numbers into stories of real human suffering and resilience. It is through this empathetic connection that society is spurred into action, mobilizing resources, and influencing policy changes.

Yet, the power of media is not wielded without responsibility. Ethical considerations must be at the forefront of any media engagement with human trafficking. Sensationalism and voyeurism can easily taint the portrayal of victims, reducing their profound suffering to mere spectacle. It is crucial, therefore, that media practitioners approach their work with a deep sense of dignity, ensuring that their narratives respect the humanity and agency of those they represent.

Digital platforms, with their expansive reach and interactive capabilities, offer new dimensions to media advocacy. Social media, podcasts, and online forums can foster communities of activists, disseminate educational resources, and provide spaces for survivor voices. The dynamics of digital sharing mean that messages can quickly amplify, challenging traditional barriers to awareness and catalyzing a global response to local instances of trafficking (Austin and Farrell, 2017).

However, the digital realm is not without its pitfalls. The same platforms that enable advocacy can also be exploited by traffickers, necessitating a nuanced understanding of the digital landscape. Media initiatives must be both vigilant and innovative, employing strategies that leverage the strengths of digital media while guarding against its vulnerabilities.

Media campaigns targeting human trafficking require a strategic blend of emotional appeal and factual accuracy. Narratives that are too heavy-handed can desensitize the audience, whereas overly didactic presentations may fail to engage. Finding this balance is crucial in crafting messages that resonate, educate, and motivate the public towards advocacy and action.

Partnerships between media outlets and anti-trafficking organizations can amplify advocacy efforts. Collaborative ventures can pool resources, expertise, and platforms, creating synergistic campaigns that harness the strengths of each partner. These alliances can also ensure that media portrayals are accurate, respectful, and aligned with the goals of anti-trafficking movements.

The power of visual media in advocacy cannot be overstated. Documentaries, photojournalism, and film have the unique ability to depict the stark realities of trafficking, making the invisible visible. These visual narratives can bypass linguistic and cultural barriers, appealing directly to the human psyche's visual processing faculties, eliciting a visceral and immediate response.

Survivor stories, when shared with respect and consent, can be particularly potent tools in media advocacy. These firsthand accounts provide authentic insight into the complexities of trafficking, challenging stereotypes and misconceptions. They also serve as powerful testimonies to resilience and recovery, offering hope and inspiring solidarity with survivors.

Measurement of media impact is essential for refining advocacy strategies. Analytics and feedback mechanisms can gauge audience engagement, sentiment, and behavioral changes induced by media campaigns. This data-driven approach enables advocates to tailor their messages, maximize their reach, and assess the efficacy of their efforts in real time.

Educational content is a vital component of media for advocacy. By incorporating information on recognizing signs of trafficking, understanding its root causes, and knowing how to respond, media can equip the public with the knowledge needed to act as first responders in their communities. Education through media thus becomes a tool for prevention and empowerment.

The interplay between media and legislation is significant. Media campaigns can inform the public about proposed laws and policies, generating public support for legislative action against trafficking. By highlighting the human stories behind the legislative process, media can bridge the gap between abstract legal reforms and their tangible impact on lives (Houston-Kolnik et al., 2020).

Finally, the spiritual dimension of media advocacy should not be overlooked. Faith-based media, by aligning with moral and ethical principles, can mobilize faith communities against trafficking. Such media can invoke themes of justice, compassion, and stewardship, rallying support from religious individuals and groups who view the fight against trafficking as part of their spiritual duty.

In conclusion, the media, with its vast capabilities, plays an indispensable role in the fight against human trafficking. Through ethical, informed, and innovative approaches, media advocacy can shed light on darkness, inspire action, and contribute significantly to the eradication of this modern-day slavery. It is a potent instrument of change, capable of mobilizing society towards a future where freedom prevails for all.

Chapter 18: Corporate Accountability and Labor Trafficking

In the ongoing effort to dismantle the scourge of human trafficking, the role of corporations in perpetuating labor trafficking through opaque supply chains and unethical sourcing strategies invites a rigorous examination. This chapter delves into the ethical responsibility corporations hold in ensuring their operations do not indirectly or directly support labor trafficking. The complexity of global supply chains often obscures the reality of labor conditions, making it imperative for corporations to implement comprehensive due diligence processes. The concept of Corporate Social Responsibility (CSR) extends beyond mere philanthropy, demanding a framework where ethical sourcing and transparency are integral to a company's operational ethos. This ethical imperative aligns with the principles of human dignity and the common good, underpinning the moral fabric of society. Research highlights the efficacy of robust regulatory frameworks and the adoption of ethical business practices in mitigating the risks of labor trafficking within supply chains (Dryhurst, 2012). Moreover, engaging consumers through transparency can foster a culture of accountability, driving demand for ethically produced goods and challenging corporations to redefine success metrics beyond the financial bottom line to include social impact (Feasley, 2016). Thus, the crusade against labor trafficking necessitates a collaborative approach, mobilizing stakeholders across sectors to forge a future where economic activity contributes to the flourishing of humanity rather than its exploitation.

Supply Chains and Ethical Sourcing

In contemporary society, the complexity of global supply chains presents a labyrinthine challenge for corporations striving to ensure ethical sourcing and corporate accountability, particularly in relation to labor trafficking. This burden is not merely a legal obligation but a moral imperative that aligns with fundamental human dignity. The weave of economic transactions across borders, the involvement of myriad entities, and the obfuscation of labor practices have rendered traditional oversight mechanisms often ineffectual, necessitating a comprehensive reevaluation of approaches to safeguarding human rights within the supply chain.

At the heart of ethical sourcing lies the stark reality of labor trafficking, a scourge that shadows the global economy. Labor trafficking, the procurement of individuals through force, fraud, or coercion for the purpose of subjection to involuntary servitude, peonage, debt bondage, or slavery, represents not merely an affront to the law but a profound ethical violation. It is a manifestation of an economy that, when left unchecked, devalues the inherent worth of the individual, reducing persons to mere instruments of profit.

Corporations, standing at the helm of global supply chains, bear a significant share of responsibility in addressing labor trafficking.

This responsibility extends beyond the confines of legality into the realm of moral duty. For every product that graces the shelves of our stores carries with it a history–a chain of human hands through which it has passed. The ethical imperative demands that these hands have worked willingly, treated with the respect and dignity that is their due (Jagers and Rijken, 2014).

The challenge, however, is monumental. Globalization has rendered supply chains increasingly opaque, with layers of subcontracting obscuring the origins of labor. Yet, this complexity cannot be an excuse for inaction. The urgency to shine a light into the shadows of supply chains, to uncover and redress any instances of labor trafficking, is paramount. This requires a concerted effort, a coalition of corporations, governments, non-governmental organizations, and civil society, each playing crucial roles in crafting a transparent, accountable, and ethically sound economic landscape.

Policy frameworks play a pivotal role in shaping corporate behaviors towards ethical sourcing. Legislation such as the Trafficking Victims Protection Act (TVPA) sets the legal foundation upon which efforts to combat labor trafficking are built. However, laws alone are insufficient. They must be underpinned by a corporate culture that prioritizes ethical considerations, that integrates respect for human dignity into the very fabric of its business operations.

Technology emerges as a potent ally in the quest for ethical sourcing. Innovative tools enable greater transparency within supply chains, facilitating the monitoring of labor practices and the verification of compliance with ethical standards. Yet, technology is a tool, not a panacea. It must be wielded with wisdom, guided by a moral compass that ensures its use serves to uplift, not to exploit (Mehra and Shay, 2016).

Consumer awareness and activism have reshaped market dynamics, compelling corporations to reckon with the ethical implications of their supply chains. The choices made by consumers, driven by an informed understanding of the impact of their purchases, wield power to catalyze change, pressuring corporations to uphold ethical sourcing practices or face economic repercussion.

Central to the discussion of ethical sourcing is the concept of human dignity. From a philosophical and theological perspective, human dignity provides the foundation upon which ethical principles are constructed. It asserts that every individual, by virtue of their humanity, is endowed with an intrinsic value that demands recognition and respect. This principle necessitates a radical reevaluation of economic systems, to ensure they serve not solely the ends of profit but the flourishing of human persons.

The integration of ethical sourcing within corporate strategies demands a multifaceted approach. It necessitates not only the establishment of rigorous auditing processes and the implementation of robust due diligence practices but also a commitment to fostering a corporate ethos that places ethical considerations at the core of decision-making processes. It is a journey that calls for perseverance, for the challenges are substantial, yet the moral imperatives are incontrovertible (Eckert, 2013).

Education and capacity building emerge as critical tools in the endeavor to promote ethical sourcing. By empowering stakeholders across the supply chain with knowledge and skills, we can build a collective resilience against the forces that perpetuate labor trafficking. It is an endeavor that requires patience, for change does not occur overnight, but with commitment and collaboration, progress is within reach.

The roadmap to ethical sourcing is fraught with challenges, yet it is a path that must be traversed. The stakes are high, for at its end lies not merely the prosperity of businesses but the welfare of countless individuals whose lives are touched by the global economy. It is a journey that calls for courage, for resilience, and, above all, for a steadfast commitment to the principles of human dignity and justice (Johnson et al., 2018).

In conclusion, the battle against labor trafficking within global supply chains is a testament to the power of collective action, a reminder of the responsibility that lies in the hands of corporations, policymakers, and individuals alike. As we forge ahead, let us be guided by a moral vision that seeks not just the absence of exploitation but the presence of justice, not merely the enforcement of laws but the enactment of ethical praxis. It is a call to action that resonates deeply with the values underpinning human dignity, a call that we must heed with unwavering determination.

Corporate Social Responsibility

In a world fraught with injustices such as labor trafficking, corporations hold a significant role in both the perpetuation of and the fight against such exploitations. The concept of Corporate Social Responsibility (CSR) has evolved from a mere buzzword to a crucial strategy in combating human rights abuses, including labor trafficking. Corporations, driven by more than profit, have the power to effect substantial change and foster an equitable society.

The importance of CSR cannot be overstated when considering the vast reach corporations have across the globe. Through ethical business practices, companies can ensure their supply chains are free from labor trafficking. This commitment to ethical sourcing not only benefits the workers in these supply chains but also enhances corporate reputations and builds trust with consumers. The moral imperative to do good while doing well encapsulates the essence of CSR in the modern commercial landscape (Lindgreen and Swaen, 2010).

However, the path to implementing effective CSR strategies is fraught with challenges. The first hurdle is the complexity of global supply chains. Transparency is often lacking, making it difficult to trace the origins of products and to ensure that all stages of production are free from exploitation. Companies must invest in rigorous audits and build relationships with suppliers that share their commitment to human rights.

Another challenge lies in the economic pressures to reduce costs, which can sometimes lead to compromised labor standards. It's a delicate balance to strike between staying competitive in the market and ensuring the ethical treatment of workers. Here, the role of consumer awareness and demand for ethically produced goods becomes paramount. As consumers become more socially conscious, they hold companies accountable, driving the latter to adopt more responsible practices (Shavers, 2012).

The implementation of CSR also extends beyond supply chain management to include corporate philanthropy, advocacy, and community engagement. Companies can leverage their resources and influence to support non-profit organizations working on the frontlines of the battle against human trafficking. Through partnerships, financial contributions, and awareness campaigns, corporations can amplify the efforts to protect vulnerable populations and dismantle trafficking networks.

Moreover, CSR should be integrated into the very fiber of corporate culture. It's not enough for CSR to be an afterthought or a department siloed from the rest of the company. Leaders must champion social responsibility and ethical practices at every level of their organization, embedding these principles into their operations, from procurement to marketing.

On a strategic level, CSR initiatives aligned with core business functions can yield synergies that benefit both the company and society. For example, companies investing in the communities where they operate, especially in developing countries, can improve social conditions while fostering a stable and prosperous environment for doing business. Education, healthcare, and economic empowerment programs can help break the cycle of poverty and reduce the vulnerability to trafficking.

The legal framework surrounding corporate accountability in issues like labor trafficking has also become more stringent. Legislation in various countries now requires companies to report on their efforts to identify and mitigate human rights abuses in their supply chains. This regulatory environment underscores the importance of proactive CSR strategies to navigate legal, ethical, and business risks.

Indeed, the road to eradicating labor trafficking is long and complex, necessitating a multifaceted approach. Corporate social responsibility offers a powerful avenue through which companies can contribute to this fight. By prioritizing ethical practices, advocating for human rights, and engaging with stakeholders, corporations can play a pivotal role in creating a more just and humane world.

Critical to this endeavor is the need for ongoing research and dialogue among businesses, non-profits, government agencies, and the public. Sharing best practices, challenges, and lessons learned can propel the collective effort to stamp out labor trafficking. It is a journey that requires persistence, innovation, and collaboration (Uduji et al., 2019).

At its core, CSR embodies the acknowledgment that business cannot thrive in a society that falters. The welfare of workers, the integrity of supply chains, and the health of communities are intricately linked to corporate success. As stewards of considerable resources and influence, companies have a moral obligation to wield their power for the greater good, championing initiatives that safeguard human dignity and promote sustainable development.

In conclusion, as we ponder the path towards eradicating labor trafficking, it's evident that corporations play a crucial role through their commitment to social responsibility. It's a testament to the notion that economic prosperity and social justice are not mutually exclusive but rather, mutually reinforcing. The call to action is clear: for corporations to rise to their full potential as agents of change in the fight against labor trafficking, embedding the principles of CSR into their DNA. In doing so, they pave the way for a future where every individual's rights are respected and protected.

Chapter 19: The Psychology of Trafficking

In delving into the abyssal depths of human trafficking's psychology, our journey is twofold: understanding the mindset of the trafficker and comprehending the consequential psychological turmoil inflicted upon the victims. Traffickers often operate under a framework of psychological manipulation and exploitation, utilizing tactics that epitomize the darkest aspects of human nature. These individuals' prey on vulnerability, employing coercion, and deceit as tools of trade, bonding their victims in invisible chains of fear and dependency. The psychological effects on victims are profound and enduring. Trauma, PTSD, depression, and a host of other mental health issues are common among those who have endured such exploitation. Researchers have documented the complex trauma experienced by trafficking victims, noting that the recovery process is often long-term and fraught with challenges (Beeson, 2014). The intertwining of psychological control with physical abuse creates a prison without bars, from which escape requires more than just physical liberation. It is a solemn reminder of our duty to not only free the physically enchained but to also embark on the arduous journey of psychological healing, underscoring the paramount importance of tailored psychological support services in the recovery process (Mordeson et al., 2022).

Understanding the Trafficker

In our journey to confront and eradicate the atrocious crime of human trafficking, it is imperative we turn our attention to those perpetuating this injustice: the traffickers themselves. Understanding the mindset, motivations, and methods of traffickers is crucial for devising effective strategies to combat trafficking. This exploration ventures deep into the psychological, societal, and economic factors that lead individuals to exploit others in such a grave manner.

Psychologically, traffickers often exhibit a disturbing detachment from empathy and moral considerations. This detachment enables them to view their victims not as fellow human beings but as commodities to be exploited for profit. Such a mindset is nurtured by societal environments where human life is undervalued, and economic disparities are rampant. The traffickers' motives are primarily driven by the lure of substantial financial gain with seemingly low risk, especially in jurisdictions where law enforcement mechanisms are weak or corruptible (Dryjanska, 2024).

The methodology of traffickers varies significantly, with some employing coercion and violence, while others use deception, promising their victims employment, education, or a better life. Understanding these methods is vital for law enforcement and communities to identify and intervene in potential trafficking situations effectively.

Traffickers often exploit vulnerabilities such as poverty, lack of education, and social or political instability. These conditions create a fertile ground for traffickers to offer false hope to those desperately seeking a way out of their situations. The complexities of trafficking necessitate a multifaceted approach in its combat, involving not only punitive measures against traffickers but also addressing the root causes that make individuals vulnerable to trafficking in the first place.

From a societal perspective, traffickers often operate within networks that can span across borders, making trafficking a highly organized and transnational crime. These networks can sometimes involve collusion with corrupt officials, complicating efforts to dismantle them. The global nature of trafficking demands international cooperation and a unified response from law enforcement agencies worldwide (Fong and Cardoso, 2010).

Despite the grim reality of their actions, some traffickers do not see themselves as perpetrators of crime but rather as businesspeople responding to supply and demand dynamics in the market. This rationalization is a stark reminder of how deeply entrenched the commodification of humans has become in certain circles. Combatting this mindset requires a cultural shift towards greater respect for human dignity and stringent enforcement of laws that protect individuals from exploitation.

Addressing the demand side of human trafficking is equally important. By reducing demand for cheap labor and services that trafficking victims are forced into, the profitability of trafficking operations can be significantly undermined, making the crime less attractive to potential traffickers. Public awareness campaigns and ethical consumerism play crucial roles in this aspect.

The role of technology in trafficking cannot be overlooked. Traffickers increasingly use the internet and social media to recruit victims and communicate with clients discreetly. This digital dimension of trafficking necessitates sophisticated technological interventions and collaborations with tech companies to monitor and intercept trafficking activities online.

Preventative measures must also focus on education and empowerment of at-risk populations. By providing access to education, employment opportunities, and social services, individuals are less likely to fall prey to traffickers' deceptions. Empowering communities to recognize and resist trafficking is a formidable barrier against traffickers.

On a legislative level, while many countries have made significant strides in enacting laws against trafficking, enforcement remains a challenge. Strengthening law enforcement agencies' capacity to tackle trafficking, ensuring the criminal justice system can appropriately prosecute traffickers, and protect victims are essential steps in this direction.

Moreover, rehabilitation and social reintegration of trafficking victims are critical. By ensuring that victims have access to justice and support services, society can deny traffickers the ability to re-victimize or use threats against victims' families as a means of control.

It's salient to note that traffickers often prey on the most marginalized segments of society — minorities, migrants, and the economically disenfranchised. Tackling human trafficking thus intersects with broader efforts to combat inequality, racism, and xenophobia.

Finally, faith-based communities and organizations play a unique role in both preventing trafficking and supporting its victims. Their moral and ethical frameworks, coupled with extensive community networks, make them invaluable allies in the fight against trafficking. Their involvement underscores the moral imperative shared across faith traditions to protect the vulnerable and pursue justice (Beeson, 2014).

In conclusion, understanding the trafficker is a complex endeavor, requiring a nuanced approach that addresses psychological, societal, and economic dimensions. It's a call to action for a collective response from law enforcement, legislators, communities, and individuals alike. Only by comprehensively understanding the forces driving traffickers can we hope to dismantle the structures that enable human trafficking and restore dignity and freedom to its countless victims.

Effects on Victims

The scourge of human trafficking, as it unfurls across the breadth of our nation, does not simply disrupt societies; it profoundly devastates the individuals caught in its grasp. Each victim, ensnared by the allure or forcefulness of traffickers, embarks on a harrowing journey marked by profound psychological, physical, and emotional scarring. To fathom the depth of this impact, one must delve into the myriad ways in which trafficking alters a person's essence, reshaping their view of the world, of others, and, most poignantly, of themselves.

The psychological effects on victims of human trafficking are both complex and multifaceted, reflecting the severe exploitation they endure. The manipulation and coercion used by traffickers often lead to a psychological phenomenon known as "learned helplessness" (Pascale et al., 2023). In this state, victims feel utterly powerless, believing that they have no control over their lives or their situation. This crippling mindset can persist long after their physical escape from trafficking, hindering recovery and integration into society.

Furthermore, post-traumatic stress disorder (PTSD) is widespread among trafficking survivors. The constant exposure to trauma, violence, and fear ingrains itself into their psyche, manifesting in nightmares, flashbacks, severe anxiety, and uncontrollable thoughts about their experiences (Jones, 2019). The battle against these symptoms is not merely a daily fight; it's a moment-to-moment struggle to reclaim peace of mind and emotional stability.

Depression is another common affliction plaguing victims of trafficking. The sense of isolation, betrayal, and worthlessness weighs heavily on their hearts, often leading to suicidal thoughts or attempts. The road to rediscovering hope, purpose, and self-worth is arduous, demanding unwavering support from the community and professionals alike.

Victims also frequently suffer from severe anxiety disorders, including generalized anxiety disorder and panic attacks. The unpredictability of their situation while being trafficked leaves a lasting mark, making them perpetually fearful of unknown and perceived threats. This state of hyper-vigilance complicates their ability to form trusting relationships and can significantly impair social and occupational functioning.

A particularly insidious effect of human trafficking is the erosion of trust. Victims often experience betrayal by those they previously trusted or were forced to place trust in their traffickers as a survival mechanism. Rebuilding this fundamental component of human relationships can be an excruciatingly slow process, requiring patience and understanding from loved ones and professionals.

The stigma associated with being a victim of trafficking further exacerbates these psychological wounds. Society's misconceptions and judgments can isolate victims, making them reluctant to seek help or share their stories. This isolation can perpetuate feelings of shame and worthlessness, deepening their trauma.

Physical health issues are also paramount, with many victims suffering from injuries inflicted by their traffickers or conditions stemming from poor living conditions and neglect. Additionally, victims of sex trafficking may face reproductive health issues, STDs, and the consequences of forced abortions, necessitating comprehensive and compassionate healthcare services (Atkins, 2008).

The cognitive impairments resulting from prolonged stress and trauma cannot be overlooked. Memory loss, difficulty concentrating, and impaired decision-making abilities are common, impacting victims' capacity to learn, work, and engage in everyday activities.

Children who fall prey to trafficking face unique challenges in their development. The exploitation disrupts their education, emotional development, and socialization, leaving lasting impacts that can alter the trajectory of their lives. The process of healing and reintegration for these young victims requires specialized interventions that address both their physical and psychological needs.

On a relational level, the effects of trafficking can sever familial and social connections, leaving victims feeling alienated from their communities. The journey towards rebuilding these relationships is fraught with challenges, as both victims and their families must navigate a complex web of emotions, including guilt, anger, and grief (Salami et al., 2018).

The economic implications for victims are also significant. Many emerge from trafficking with no financial resources, education, or professional skills, making it difficult to achieve economic independence and stability. This vulnerability can lead to re-victimization or force individuals into precarious situations to survive.

However, amidst these myriad challenges, there lies a potential pathway to resilience and recovery. With appropriate support, victims can begin to heal the psychological wounds inflicted by trafficking. By fostering a sense of empowerment and rebuilding their lives with dignity and purpose, survivors can transform their painful experiences into a source of strength.

The role of faith and spirituality in this healing process cannot be underestimated. For many victims, reconnecting with their faith or exploring spiritual practices can offer solace, hope, and a renewed sense of belonging. In this light, spiritual communities have the potential to play a pivotal role in supporting survivors on their journey towards healing and redemption.

In conclusion, the effects of human trafficking on its victims are profound and enduring. Yet, through a comprehensive approach that addresses psychological, physical, economic, and spiritual needs, recovery is possible. It is incumbent upon society to extend empathy, support, and resources to these individuals, enabling them to reclaim their lives and emerge stronger in the aftermath of their ordeal.

Chapter 20: Special Focus: Children in Trafficking

The vile entrapment of children within the shadowed realms of human trafficking is a scourge that afflicts the most innocent among us. These young souls, coerced or kidnapped into situations of exploitation, face not only the loss of their freedom but an indelible impact on their development and psyche. The dynamics of child trafficking are both complex and heart-wrenching. Predators exploit the vulnerability of children, often using manipulation or outright force to ensnare them into various forms of servitude-be it for labor, sexual exploitation, or other illegal activities (Rafferty, 2008). The innocence of childhood is corrupted, twisted into a commodity that traffickers trade with cold calculation.

Efforts to shield and recover these young victims are multifaceted, requiring a blend of vigilance, compassion, and decisive action. Protective measures are essential in preventing the trafficking of children, integrating community awareness programs, school-based initiatives, and rigorous enforcement of laws designed to deter traffickers. Recovery and reintegration programs play a critical role in healing the wounds inflicted by trafficking. These programs must address the physical, emotional, and psychological harm suffered by children caught in these atrocious situations, offering them a pathway to reclaim their lives and hope for a future (Nazer and Greenbaum, 2020).

Engagement from every sector of society is vital in eradicating the trafficking of children. Law enforcement agencies, educational institutions, healthcare providers, and community organizations must unite in a common purpose to detect, prevent, and combat this form of modern-day slavery. Faith-based communities, in particular, can provide a sanctuary for healing and recovery, leveraging their moral influence and resources in support of these vulnerable children. Only through concerted effort can we hope to dismantle the networks that perpetuate child trafficking and restore the rights and dignity of its youngest victims (Raffert, 2021).

Child Trafficking Dynamics

The phenomenon of child trafficking, in its manifold dimensions, intertwines with the basest instincts of exploitation and the highest callings for justice and protection of the innocent. Within the context of the United States, this scourge manifests through various forms, transforming the lives of its victims into narratives of despair and, for the fortunate few, resilience and recovery. The dynamics of child trafficking are complex, driven by demand and facilitated by the vulnerability of the young and the marginalized.

Central to understanding these dynamics is recognizing the factors that render children susceptible. Poverty, family instability, and lack of education form a triad of vulnerability, making children susceptible to the false promises of traffickers. These perpetrators exploit the innocence and trust inherent in children, weaving webs of deception that lead away from home and into the throes of exploitation (Suvaningsi et al., 2021).

In the American context, the internet has emerged as a predominant arena for the trafficking of children. Traffickers deftly navigate social media platforms, gaming sites, and chat rooms, masquerading as friends and confidantes to lure children into their traps. The digital age, for all its benefits, has thus paradoxically heightened the risks children face, expanding the reach of traffickers beyond physical spaces and into virtual ones.

Once entrapped, the experiences of trafficked children are marked by profound exploitation and abuse. The forms of trafficking they endure are multifaceted, ranging from forced labor in agricultural or domestic realms to sexual exploitation. The latter is particularly heinous, with children being coerced into performing in pornographic materials or provided to adults seeking illicit encounters. The commodification of their innocence stands as a stark testament to the depravity of traffickers (Querol and Lerner, 2021).

The trafficking of children is not merely an act of individual malice but is sustained by a broader societal demand for exploitable labor and sexual exploitation. This demand creates a market in which children are viewed and treated as commodities, their worth tied to their utility to traffickers and those who avail themselves of trafficked services. It's a chilling reflection of societal failings and a clear indicator of the systemic underpinnings of this crime.

Confronting this crisis requires a multifaceted response that addresses both the supply and demand sides of trafficking. Law enforcement plays a crucial role in apprehending and prosecuting traffickers, dismantling the networks that perpetuate this crime. Yet, prosecution alone is insufficient. Preventive measures, focused on education and awareness, are vital in curtailing the vulnerability of children to trafficking's allure. Moreover, societal attitudes towards consumption patterns that indirectly perpetuate labor and sexual exploitation must be scrutinized and reformed.

Protection and recovery measures for victims are paramount. The journey from victim to survivor is fraught with challenges, both psychological and physical. Recovering from the trauma of trafficking requires an ecosystem of support, including mental health services, education, and integration opportunities. The path to healing is often long and complex, highlighting the importance of dedicated resources and empathetic, comprehensive care approaches (Hart, 2008).

The role of community and faith-based organizations in supporting recovery and raising awareness cannot be overstated. In providing a network of support and advocacy, they embody the principles of compassion and justice central to the fight against child trafficking. Their efforts underscore the necessity of collective action in confronting this evil.

Addressing child trafficking also demands a reckoning with broader societal issues that fuel its persistence. Economic disparities, social injustice, and the erosion of community and familial structures all contribute to the environment in which trafficking thrives. Tackling these root causes is essential in fostering a society where children are safe from the clutches of traffickers.

Education, both of the public and of vulnerable populations, emerges as a powerful tool in the arsenal against trafficking. Awareness campaigns that elucidate the signs of trafficking and educate on online safety can significantly mitigate the risks children face. Schools, as centers of learning and development, hold a particular responsibility in integrating these discussions into their curricula, equipping children with the knowledge and skills to navigate an increasingly complex world.

Legislation, while an essential deterrent, must be continually evaluated and updated in response to the evolving tactics of traffickers. The nimbleness of trafficking networks, particularly in their utilization of technology, calls for equally adaptive legal frameworks and enforcement strategies. State and federal laws must align to offer no quarter to traffickers while ensuring robust protections for victims.

Child trafficking, with all its complexities, is an affront to the inherent dignity and worth of every child. It strips the young of their innocence, their freedom, and their future, constituting a grave violation of human rights and an egregious offense against decency and morality. The fight against this scourge is a testament to the resilience of the human spirit and the enduring belief in the possibility of justice and renewal.

In sum, the dynamics of child trafficking require a response that is as multifaceted and adaptive as the crime itself. It is a battle that must be waged on various fronts: legal, educational, societal, and moral. By standing united in this fight, informed by the principles of justice and compassion, society can forge a path towards the eradication of this evil, restoring hope and dignity to the lives of affected children.

Protective and Recovery Measures

In the quest to confront and overcome the scourge of trafficking, particularly as it affects the most vulnerable among us-our children-the necessity for robust protective and recovery measures cannot be overstated. The welfare and restoration of these young victims form a cornerstone upon which the broader fight against human trafficking rests. In this light, efforts at safeguarding children and facilitating their healing must be both comprehensive and multifaceted, blending legal, psychological, and social strategies to address the complex needs of those affected.

Firstly, from a legal perspective, there is an imperative need for child-specific legislation that not only penalizes traffickers with the utmost severity but also provides for the unique needs of child victims. Such legislation must consider the long-lasting trauma experienced by these children and, therefore, include provisions for their physical, psychological, and social rehabilitation (Rafferty, 2008). This approach underscores the fundamental principle that children are not mere witnesses to or objects within these crimes but are individuals with inherent rights deserving of full protection and support.

Pertinently, the protection of children from trafficking begins with the establishment of robust mechanisms for their identification. Given their vulnerability and the manipulative tactics often employed by traffickers, children may not readily identify themselves as victims. Consequently, training for law enforcement, healthcare providers, educators, and other frontline professionals is essential to spot the subtle signs of trafficking and initiate appropriate interventions (Querol and Lerner, 2021).

Upon identification, immediate measures to ensure the child's safety are critical. Safe housing that is not only secure but also conducive to healing, is a primary requirement. These environments must be staffed with professionals skilled in trauma-informed care, recognizing the profound impacts of trafficking on a child's mental and physical wellbeing (Aliotta, 2021).

The journey towards recovery is invariably a long and complex one, necessitating a spectrum of therapeutic interventions. Psychological support, including trauma-focused cognitive behavioral therapy, can help children process their experiences and begin rebuilding their sense of self-worth and agency. Moreover, education and vocational training are vital components of recovery programs, offering survivors pathways to rebuild their lives and break the cycle of exploitation.

In parallel, efforts to reintegrate child victims into society must be handled with sensitivity and care. The stigma associated with trafficking can lead to social isolation, complicating recovery. Community-based support programs that foster understanding and acceptance are indispensable in ensuring that children can return to a semblance of normalcy.

Equally important is the role of the familial unit in the recovery process. While not always feasible or appropriate, the reintegration of children with their families, where safe and beneficial for the child, should be pursued. Support and counseling for families are crucial, equipping them with the knowledge and resources to provide a supportive home environment.

Preventative measures, though not directly part of the recovery process, are intrinsically linked to the protection of children from trafficking. Education and awareness-raising initiatives targeting children, families, and communities at large play a vital role in prevention. Empowering children with knowledge about trafficking, including how to recognize and report potential threats, is a fundamental safeguard against exploitation.

In concert with these frontline efforts, policy advocacy is instrumental in driving systemic change. Advocacy for policies that enhance child protection, support victims, and ensure rigorous prosecution of traffickers is essential to a comprehensive anti-trafficking strategy. This requires a unified effort among government entities, nonprofit organizations, faith groups, and the broader community.

On a practical level, the sustainability of protective and recovery programs hinges on adequate funding and resources. Securing ongoing support for these initiatives is a challenge that necessitates innovative approaches to philanthropy, government funding, and public-private partnerships.

Ultimately, the measure of success in protecting and recovering child victims of trafficking will be found in the restoration of their dignity, autonomy, and hope for the future. It is a task of profound moral and societal import, demanding commitment, compassion, and courage from all sectors of society.

In conclusion, the path from victimhood to empowerment for children who have suffered the indignities of trafficking is fraught with challenges. Yet, with a concerted and holistic approach, embodying legal protection, psychological healing, and societal reintegration, there is hope. As a community united in purpose and action, we hold the power to not only mend broken lives but also to forge a future where children are shielded from the horrors of trafficking.

Chapter 21: Engaging Faith Communities

In the ongoing struggle to dismantle the deeply entrenched networks of human trafficking within America, the mobilization of faith communities emerges as a pivotal frontier. Grounded in a profound commitment to dignity, justice, and compassion, these communities wield a unique influence capable of inspiring transformative change. This chapter delves into the strategic engagement of churches and faith groups, elucidating how their doctrinal beliefs and societal reach can be harnessed to combat trafficking effectively. Recognizing that spiritual healing forms an integral component of recovery for many survivors, faith-based healing programs are highlighted for their holistic approach, addressing the psychological and spiritual wounds inflicted by trafficking. The collaborative efforts between faith communities and secular anti-trafficking organizations are examined, showcasing successful models of partnership that amplify impact through shared resources and expertise (Smith, 2019). Furthermore, the chapter explores the theological underpinnings that motivate and sustain faith-based activism, providing a robust framework for understanding the moral imperatives driving this crucial work (Johnson & O'Brien, 2021). As faith communities continue to galvanize, their role in raising awareness, supporting survivors, and advocating for systemic change represents a beacon of hope in the fight against trafficking, reinforcing the belief that collective action rooted in faith can pave the way toward a future free from exploitation (Atkins, 2008).

Mobilizing Churches and Faith Groups

The battle against human trafficking is a complex and formidable one, requiring the concerted efforts of many facets of society. Among these, churches and faith groups hold a unique and powerful position. Their deep community roots, moral authority, and extensive networks make them vital allies in this fight. This section explores the critical role that churches and faith groups can play in mobilizing against human trafficking and outlines practical steps that can be taken to make a tangible impact.

Firstly, awareness creation stands as a foundational step. Many faithful are unaware of the extent to which human trafficking pervades their communities. Churches can serve as platforms for education, employing sermons, workshops, and informational materials to illuminate the pernicious reality of trafficking. Through fostering an informed congregation, churches set the stage for a proactive rather than reactive approach to combating trafficking.

Moreover, training is an essential component of mobilization. Clergy and lay leaders alike benefit from specialized training on identifying signs of trafficking and appropriate responses. Such training, often provided in partnership with experts and organizations experienced in anti-trafficking efforts, equips faith communities with the knowledge and tools needed for early detection and intervention.

One significant asset that churches possess is their ability to offer comprehensive support to survivors. Faith groups can harness their vast resources to provide essential services such as counseling, safe housing, legal assistance, and job training. The compassionate and welcoming environment of faith communities offers survivors a safe haven where they can find healing and restoration.

Furthermore, advocacy is a powerful avenue through which churches can effect change. By leveraging their collective voice, faith groups can influence policy at local, state, and national levels. Campaigns and petitions led by churches can urge lawmakers to enact and enforce laws that protect victims and punish traffickers. Faith communities can also engage in public awareness campaigns, using their reach to educate the wider community and rally support for eradication efforts.

Partnerships with law enforcement are essential for the successful apprehension and prosecution of traffickers. Churches can foster relationships with local police departments and federal agencies, facilitating training for officers on cultural competency and the specific needs of survivors within faith contexts. These partnerships enhance the effectiveness of investigations and ensure that victims receive the care and support they need.

International collaboration further extends the reach of churches in combating trafficking. Many faith organizations span across countries, uniquely positioning them to aid in the global fight against trafficking. Collaborating with faith groups in other nations allows for cross-border support, information sharing, and efforts to dismantle international trafficking networks.

Prevention is another critical area where churches can make a significant impact. By integrating discussions on human dignity, respect, and the evils of exploitation into faith-based education programs, churches can cultivate a culture that stands firmly against trafficking. Youth groups, in particular, provide a valuable platform for engaging the younger generation in discussions about justice, compassion, and their role in preventing trafficking.

Volunteer mobilization within congregations can provide the manpower needed for various anti-trafficking initiatives. Churches can organize volunteer teams to support local shelters, participate in community outreach, or even form watchdog groups that monitor for potential trafficking activities in their locales.

Financial contributions and fundraising within faith communities can significantly bolster the efforts of organizations dedicated to combating trafficking. By offering financial support, churches can help these organizations expand their reach and enhance their impact.

In addressing the needs of marginalized populations, churches can tackle one of the root causes of trafficking. Offering support services to at-risk groups reduces their vulnerability to traffickers. Initiatives may include food pantries, job training programs, and support for immigrants and refugees.

Interfaith initiatives are vital in building a united front against trafficking. Given the universal condemnation of trafficking by all major religions, interfaith collaborations can amplify efforts, pooling resources and knowledge for greater impact.

Spiritual support for survivors is an area where faith communities excel. Offering pastoral care, prayer groups, and spiritual counseling, churches can address the profound emotional and spiritual wounds inflicted by trafficking. This spiritual nourishment is integral to the holistic healing process for survivors.

Finally, faith groups can lead by example, implementing ethical practices within their operations to ensure they're not inadvertently supporting trafficking. This includes scrutinizing supply chains for church goods and ensuring fair labor practices in church-affiliated businesses.

In conclusion, mobilizing churches and faith groups against human trafficking is not merely an option; it's a moral imperative. By educating congregants, supporting survivors, advocating for justice, and fostering international and interfaith collaborations, faith communities can drive significant progress in the fight against this scourge. As members of a global community called to uphold the dignity of every human being, the charge to combat trafficking is a sacred duty that churches are uniquely equipped to undertake.

Faith-Based Healing Programs

The previous chapters have laid out the stark reality and multifaceted nature of human trafficking as a blight upon our society. It is within this context that faith communities, particularly the Catholic Church, find themselves called to action, not only in prevention and education but significantly in the healing and restoration of survivors. This chapter delves into the critical role of Faith-Based Healing Programs, operationalized through the lens of compassion, communal support, and spiritual renewal.

In addressing the aftermath of trafficking, the psychological and spiritual wounds inflicted upon victims are profound and complex. Secular counseling and support mechanisms, while critical, can sometimes overlook the spiritual despair that many survivors contend with. Herein lies the indispensable role of faith-based healing programs which offer a holistic approach to recovery, addressing both the corporeal and spiritual dimensions of healing.

These programs function under the tenet of imago Dei, the belief that every individual is made in the image of God and, as such, possesses intrinsic dignity and worth (Genesis 1:27). This principle undergirds the therapeutic efforts, instilling in survivors a sense of self-worth and belonging that trafficking had stripped away.

Moreover, faith-based programs often operate within existing church networks, harnessing a community-oriented approach to healing. This communal aspect is vital, as the isolation experienced during and after trafficking can be profoundly debilitating. The sense of belonging to a community, of being seen, heard, and valued, can be transformative for survivors, fostering resilience and facilitating more profound healing.

One of the core components of these programs is their emphasis on spiritual counseling and guidance. The traumas of trafficking can leave survivors questioning their faith, feeling abandoned by God, or unworthy of His love. Spiritual counseling offers a pathway through these spiritual crises, helping survivors reconcile their experiences with their faith, often through the narratives of redemption, forgiveness, and hope found in scripture.

It's imperative to note that while these programs are deeply rooted in faith, they are inclusive and respectful of the survivors' spiritual beliefs and trajectories. The objective is not conversion but healing, marked by an ethos of 'meeting people where they are' and accompanying them on their journey toward recovery.

The effectiveness of faith-based healing programs, however, is not solely a matter of spiritual intervention. Many work in tandem with professional mental health services, recognizing the importance of a multidisciplinary approach to healing. This symbiotic relationship between faith and science underscores the programs' holism, aiming for the restoration of the whole person.

Case studies and testimonials from survivors who have participated in these programs speak volumes about their impact. Many recount experiences of profound spiritual renewal, of finding hope amidst despair, and of beginning to envision a future free from the chains of their past. These stories are powerful testaments to the transformative power of faith-based healing in the lives of trafficking survivors.

Yet, the journey is not without its challenges. Stigma, both within and outside the church, can be a significant barrier to accessing these programs. There remains a pressing need for continued education and advocacy within faith communities to dismantle misconceptions around human trafficking and to cultivate a culture of openness and support.

Furthermore, the scalability and sustainability of these programs are contingent upon robust support networks and resources. The involvement of the broader church community, through volunteering, fundraising, and advocacy, is essential in ensuring these programs can reach and support as many survivors as possible.

In conclusion, faith-based healing programs embody the compassionate and redemptive heart of the faith community's response to human trafficking. They stand as beacons of hope, offering a path to healing that is steeped in the love and dignity that every person deserves. As such, they are a vital component of the collective effort required to address the scourge of human trafficking, heralding a future where freedom and healing are possible for all.

References:

Chapter 22: Roman Catholic Prayers Against Trafficking

In this critical juncture of our battle against the scourge of human trafficking, we turn to a unique arsenal - the power of prayer within the Roman Catholic faith. Recognizing the profound impacts of spiritual warfare against the darkness of human trafficking, this chapter delineates the essence of invoking divine intervention through prayers of adoration, contrition, thanksgiving, and supplication. The theological foundation of such prayers lies not only in beseeching God's intercession but also in fortifying the communal resolve against the atrocities of trafficking. Prayers of adoration acknowledge the sovereignty of God over all creations, including the intricacies of human freedom and dignity. Through prayers of contrition, the faithful express remorse for societal sins that have allowed such evils to fester. Thanksgiving prayers serve as reminders of the victories, both big and small, against trafficking, celebrating every soul rescued and every perpetrator brought to justice. Lastly, prayers of supplication are fervent appeals for the protection of the vulnerable, the liberation of those ensnared, and the conversion of those who perpetrate these crimes.

Prayers of Adoration

In the overwhelming shadow of human trafficking that darkens the corners of our world, we, as believers and steadfast participants in the Catholic faith, find solace and strength in prayers of adoration. This intrinsic aspect of our prayer life allows us not only to acknowledge the infinite majesty and mercy of our Creator but also to lay the groundwork for our petition against the grievance of trafficking that afflicts countless souls. In moments of adoration, we lift our hearts and minds to God, recognizing His sovereignty and imploring His intervention in the plight of those ensnared by the chains of modern-day slavery.

The act of adoration, in its purest form, serves as a sanctified offering that transcends the physical realm, an ethereal connection between the divine and the mortal. It is in this sacred space that we as the faithful, guided by the Holy Spirit, can offer up our prayers for the victims of trafficking, identifying with their suffering through the passion of Christ our Savior. Through our prayers of adoration, we affirm that God's love knows no bounds, and His justice no limitation. We acknowledge that in the face of such profound evil, our Almighty Father remains an unyielding beacon of hope and redemption for all.

Let us, therefore, in our prayers of adoration, elevate the dignity of every human being, recognizing each person as a masterpiece of God's creation, inherently worthy of respect, love, and freedom. By doing so, we not only honor the divine image in which we are all made but also confront the injustice of trafficking with the profound power of divine love.

In these moments of spiritual reflection and adoration, let us recall the words of Scripture, which remind us that "The Lord is good to all, and his mercy is over all that he has made" (Psalm 145:9). This divine goodness and mercy inspire us to advocate relentlessly for those trapped in the darkness of trafficking, empowering us to be instruments of God's light.

Our adoration extends beyond words, transforming into actions that mirror the love of Christ, who came "to proclaim freedom for the prisoners and recovery of sight for the blind, to set the oppressed free" (Luke 4:18). As his followers, we are called to embody this mission in our fight against trafficking, inspired by our adoration of the God who desires freedom for all His children.

Let our prayers of adoration reinvigorate our commitment to this cause, fueling our efforts with the knowledge that with God, all things are possible. In the face of such adversity, our faith provides the assurance that darkness can never overcome the light of Christ, which shines brightly within every action taken to combat trafficking.

As we continue to navigate the complexities and challenges of battling human trafficking, our adoration becomes a cornerstone of hope, not just for us but for every soul longing for liberation. In our profound reverence and worship, we find the strength to persevere, the courage to speak out, and the wisdom to act justly.

In this sacred dialogue of adoration, we are reminded of our collective responsibility to safeguard the sanctity of human life and dignity. It compels us to look beyond our own needs, to reach out to those who suffer in silence, and to be their voice when they cannot speak. Our adoration, therefore, becomes an act of solidarity, a testament to our unwavering belief in the power of God's grace to heal, restore, and redeem.

Therefore, let us approach our prayers of adoration with heartfelt reverence, mindful of their profound impact on our spiritual journey and our mission to end human trafficking. Through these prayers, we not only glorify God but also affirm our dedication to the cause of justice and mercy, standing in firm opposition to every form of oppression.

In conclusion, our prayers of adoration are not passive utterances but dynamic expressions of faith that propel us towards consequential action against trafficking. They anchor us in the truth of God's love, equip us with divine courage, and unite us in a common purpose to restore freedom and dignity to the oppressed. May our adoration reflect the depth of our compassion, the breadth of our commitment, and the strength of our resolve to bring an end to human trafficking, offering a beacon of hope to those who endure its chains.

Prayers of Contrition

In the face of human trafficking's horror, it is paramount that we, as individuals and collectively as a faith community, step forth in humility and contrition. Acknowledging our failings and the ways in which society has permitted such atrocities to fester is the first step toward healing and redemption. Human trafficking, in its vile disregard for the sanctity of human life, presents a stark counterpoint to the Gospel's message of love, freedom, and dignity for all.

Prayer, particularly prayers of contrition, are not merely expressions of sorrow; they are commitments to change, to act justly, and to live out the teachings of our faith that respect the inherent value of every person. In turning to God with a contrite heart, we recognize our participation, whether direct or indirect, in societal sins that allow slavery to persist in modern forms.

It is said that a humble and contrite heart, God will not despise (Psalm 51:17). In this spirit, our prayers of contrition on behalf of the victims of trafficking are more than personal catharsis; they are cries for divine intervention in a world marred by exploitation. They are an admission of our collective weakness and a plea for the strength to fight this evil with all the means at our disposal.

Our prayers thus turn towards the Lord, asking for forgiveness for when we have turned a blind eye to the suffering of our brothers and sisters ensnared in trafficking. For all the times we have failed to see Christ in the least of His children, for the moments we chose comfort and convenience over courageous action against injustice, we seek mercy.

In these prayers, we also seek wisdom – to recognize trafficking in our midst, the insight to see beyond the surface, and the understanding that our actions or inactions play a role in perpetuating this scourge. Such prayers are a beacon of light in the darkness that trafficking casts over its victims, a declaration of our commitment to see, to speak, and to act.

To combat human trafficking effectively, our prayers of contrition must move us to concrete action. As the body of Christ on Earth, we are called to be the hands and feet of Jesus, actively working to liberate those held in bondage. In praying, let us also ask for the courage to step out of our comfort zones, to advocate for change, and to support the organizations dedicated to ending trafficking.

As members of a global Roman Catholic community, our interconnectedness necessitates a universal commitment to fighting this injustice. Our prayers link us with the suffering of trafficking victims worldwide, reminding us that they, too, are part of Christ's body. Through our collective prayers and actions, we contribute to a tidal wave of change against the forces of evil that traffic human beings.

In our parishes and communities, let us therefore incorporate prayers of contrition not as occasional practices but as essential elements of our worship and reflection. In doing so, we cultivate a communal heart that is continually broken by the injustices of our world but is also perpetually hopeful in the power of God to bring about redemption and healing.

Embedded within the heart of Catholic social teaching is the call to uphold the dignity of every human being. Our prayers of contrition for the sin of human trafficking reaffirm this foundational belief and recommit us to the Church's mission to serve the least among us. In these prayers, we find the synthesis of divine grace and human responsibility, a potent force for change in our troubled world.

Moreover, let these prayers be a source of solace for the victims of trafficking. May they feel the presence of a loving and compassionate God through the actions inspired by our heartfelt contrition. May they know that they are not forgotten, that across the world, Catholics are praying for their release, recovery, and rehabilitation.

Indeed, prayers of contrition are just the beginning. They awake our consciences, stir our compassion, and energize our resolve to act. Addressing human trafficking requires our sustained attention, resources, and commitment to justice and freedom as expressions of our faith.

Therefore, let us approach the altar with heavy hearts but also with a spirit of resolve. We pray for forgiveness, for the strength to confront this evil, and for the wisdom to support survivors in their journey of healing. And in our prayers, let us always remember the transformative power of God's love to bring about restoration and peace where there is brokenness and conflict.

May our prayers of contrition, then, not be seen as mere utterances but as catalysts for action, propelling the Church and its faithful towards tireless work in eradicating human trafficking from the face of the Earth. Together, through prayer and action, we can make a difference.

So, as we continue to navigate the complexities of addressing human trafficking, let our prayers of contrition guide us towards a future where all God's children live in dignity, free from the chains of oppression. Let it be a future we actively help to create, fueled by our faith, hope, and love.

Prayers of Thanksgiving

In the midst of the harrowing journey to eradicate human trafficking, it's essential to pause and offer prayers of thanksgiving. These prayers serve as beacons of light, reminding us of the divine grace that guides our actions and sustains our spirits. As advocates, law enforcement officials, politicians, and devout members of the Roman Catholic faith, it is our duty to recognize and give thanks for every step made towards freedom and dignity for all God's children.

Firstly, we give thanks for the resilience of the survivors. Their strength offers a testament to the indomitable spirit bestowed upon us by the Creator. Each tale of escape, recovery, and transformation is a miracle to behold and deserving of our deepest gratitude. These stories not only inspire but also illuminate the path for others still ensnared by the chains of trafficking.

We also express our profound thankfulness for the community of advocates and organizations fighting tirelessly against human trafficking. From the national platforms like Polaris Project and Shared Hope International to faith-based initiatives such as Catholic Charities and Sisters of Mercy, their collective efforts signify the human capacity for compassion and justice. Their dedication ensures that the plight of the trafficked is brought to light and addressed with the seriousness it demands.

Gratitude is extended to the legal and law enforcement communities who are at the forefront of this battle. The complexity of prosecuting traffickers and dismantling networks requires wisdom, courage, and perseverance. We are thankful for their commitment to upholding justice and for every case that leads to the conviction of traffickers and the liberation of victims.

Our thanks are similarly owed to the educators and healthcare professionals who play critical roles in prevention and recovery. Their ability to recognize signs of trafficking and provide support to those affected is invaluable. Through their dedication, they not only save lives but also empower survivors with the tools for a new beginning.

In the political arena, we give thanks for the policymakers and advocates who strive to strengthen legislation and increase awareness. Their endeavors to create environments that are hostile to trafficking but supportive of survivors are crucial for the systemic change required to end this scourge.

We are also grateful for the technological advancements and those who harness them in the fight against trafficking. Innovations in surveillance, victim identification, and global communication are pivotal elements in this contemporary battlefield. They offer hope for more effective strategies to prevent trafficking and bring perpetrators to justice.

Our prayers of thanksgiving include acknowledgment of the international collaboration combating trafficking. The partnerships formed across borders reflect a united stand against an issue that knows no boundaries. This global solidarity is a source of hope and strength, enabling shared strategies and resources to combat trafficking more effectively.

The engaging of faith communities in this cause is yet another reason for our gratitude. The mobilization of churches and faith groups adds a profound spiritual dimension to the fight against trafficking. Their commitment to healing, advocacy, and education is a powerful force for change, driven by the conviction of faith.

We give thanks for the survivors who bravely share their stories, offering insight and hope to others. Their voices are instrumental in educating the public, influencing policy, and ensuring that the realities of trafficking are neither ignored nor forgotten.

Lastly, we are thankful for every individual who, moved by empathy and justice, contributes to this cause in their unique way. Whether through volunteering, educating, donating, or simply praying, each action adds to the collective effort to terminate human trafficking.

As we proceed with our work, let these prayers of thanksgiving remind us of the progress we've made and the goodness that exists amid the darkness. It's a reminder that in our fight against human trafficking, we are never alone—divine providence guides us, survivors inspire us, and a community of compassionate individuals stands with us.

In closing, we offer our profound thanks for the opportunity to serve in this capacity, working towards a future where freedom and dignity are unassailable rights for all. May our efforts be blessed and our resolve strengthened as we continue this sacred mission.

Prayers of Supplication

In the collective effort against human trafficking, it is essential to anchor our actions in spiritual reflection and prayer. The tradition of the Roman Catholic Church offers a deep well of resources for engaging with the divine, specifically through prayers of supplication. These prayers are petitions for the Lord's intercession, guidance, and aid in the monumental task of eradicating trafficking from our midst.

Prayers of supplication within the context of combating human trafficking are not mere recitations but are profound dialogues with the Creator, seeking not only intervention but the strength to be Christ's hands and feet in the world. They implore the Almighty to awaken in every heart a fierce compassion and unwavering resolve.

One foundational prayer of supplication starts with acknowledging the imago Dei, the image of God, embedded within every human being. This recognition is vital, for it lays the ground for understanding the grievous sin of human trafficking. By praying, we petition for the courage and discernment to see this divine image in everyone, especially those most vulnerable to exploitation.

Furthermore, these prayers often entail a plea for the enlightenment of those ensnared in the operations of trafficking

– the perpetrators themselves. The appeal is for their conversion and transformation, that they might turn from their ways and recognize the profound harm they inflict. This aspect of supplication embraces the possibility of redemption and aligns with the Church's teachings on forgiveness and the potential for change.

In addressing the victims of trafficking, prayers of supplication lay bare the heart's deepest cry for their liberation, healing, and restoration. They beseech the Lord to provide solace, strength, and a path to recovery for these individuals, enveloping them in a compassionate community that mirrors Christ's love and mercy.

Additionally, these prayers often extend to those engaged in the frontline battle against trafficking - the law enforcement officers, social workers, educators, and numerous volunteers. They seek divine protection, wisdom, and perseverance for these individuals as they navigate the complexities and dangers inherent in this fight.

Prayers of supplication also touch upon the systemic and structural evils that fuel human trafficking, such as poverty, inequality, and corruption. They implore the Lord to inspire societal change, guiding politicians, lawmakers, and leaders in creating just and compassionate systems that uphold the dignity of every person.

One such prayer might include a fervent request for the illumination of consciences, leading to a global awakening to the horrors of trafficking. It petitions for a united front, composed of individuals, communities, and nations, to combat this scourge effectively.

Moreover, these prayers recognize the role of the Church and her members in addressing this issue. They call for the Holy Spirit's guidance in mobilizing the Church to be a beacon of hope, a source of comfort, and a catalyst for change in the world.

The act of offering supplications for the end of trafficking is also a humble acknowledgment of our reliance on God's grace. It admits the limitations of human effort and seeks the divine power that can bring about genuine transformation.

One critical aspect of these prayers is their communal nature. While individual prayer is powerful, gathering together in prayer magnifies our petitions, creating a unified spiritual plea that transcends boundaries. Such collective supplication has the potential to forge a stronger collective conscience and amplify the call for action.

Lastly, prayers of supplication for the cessation of trafficking are prayers of hope. They affirm our belief in a God who hears, who cares, and who acts. They sustain us in our work, reminding us that, though the night may be dark, the light of Christ's resurrection promises victory over every form of bondage and oppression.

In conclusion, prayers of supplication are an indispensable weapon in the fight against human trafficking. They ground us in our faith, unite us in our purpose, and empower us to act with divine strength. May these prayers continue to rise as incense before the Lord, leading us onward in the mission to set the captives free.

References:

Chapter 23: Taking Action: A Practical Guide

In the preceding cadences of our discourse, we've traversed the somber territories of human trafficking's landscape within America, examining its insidious forms, legislative responses, and the collective outcry for justice that resounds within the hearts of the devout, the educator, the enforcer of law, and beyond. Now, as we step into the realm of proactive engagement, it's incumbent upon us to bear the torch of action with a pragmatic fervor. The call to action is not merely a whisper in the corridors of power or within the sanctuaries of faith but a clarion call that demands a strategic, unified response from all sectors of society. Engaging in this battle against the scourge of trafficking necessitates not only understanding and empathy but a well-sprung reservoir of action-oriented strategies. Individuals are beckoned to transcend passive concern, mobilizing resources, knowledge, and networks to forge intervention pathways, enlighten communities, and safeguard the vulnerable. Organizing community action is not an insurmountable task but rather a meticulously layered strategy that calls for the synthesis of grassroots movements, faith-based initiatives, and cross-sector alliances that harness collective strengths and insights to dismantle trafficking networks and restore dignity to survivors (Smith & John, 2022). Such endeavors are underpinned by a profound commitment to the sanctity of human dignity, echoing the foundational tenets of our societies and faiths that every soul is of immeasurable worth and deserving of liberation from the fetters of exploitation.

How Individuals Can Make a Difference

In the face of the profound darkness that is human trafficking, the role of the individual in combating this scourge cannot be understated. Each person, regardless of their state in life—be it a devout Roman Catholic, a college professor, a member of law enforcement, a politician, a lawyer, or a life advocate—holds within their grasp the potential to affect meaningful change. This power to bring about transformation stems not from the grandiosity of the actions taken, but from the moral and ethical conviction behind them.

Understanding the gravity of human trafficking is the foundation upon which individuals can build their responses. It is a crime that dehumanizes its victims, treating them as commodities rather than as the dignified beings they are. Such an understanding should prompt a moral outrage, an unyielding resolve to act. This resolve is supported by the teachings of the Church, which uphold the inherent dignity of every human being and call upon the faithful to protect the vulnerable.

One of the first steps an individual can take is educating themselves and others about the realities of human trafficking. Knowledge is a potent tool in the fight against trafficking. By learning the signs and symptoms of trafficking victims, individuals empower themselves and their communities to identify potential cases and respond appropriately. Resources for such education are plentiful, including materials provided by organizations like Polaris Project and Shared Hope International.

Prayer should not be underestimated as a source of strength and intervention. For the faithful, prayer is both a shield and a sword. It fortifies the spirit and petitions divine assistance in the liberation of captives. Engaging in Roman Catholic prayers specifically against trafficking can unite communities in a spiritual battle against this evil.

Legislatively, individuals have a voice that can—and should—be used to advocate for stronger protections against human trafficking and better support for its victims. Whether through direct dialogue, writing to representatives, or participating in advocacy campaigns, there is a multitude of ways to effect legislative change. Politicians and lawyers, in particular, can leverage their professional platforms to promote laws that address the root causes of trafficking and improve the effectiveness of the justice system in prosecuting traffickers.

Volunteerism offers a hands-on approach to making a difference. Numerous organizations, including faith-based groups like Catholic Charities and Sisters of Mercy, operate initiatives aimed at preventing trafficking and assisting victims. By volunteering time, skills, or resources, individuals can directly contribute to the ongoing efforts to combat trafficking.

Professionals across various fields can incorporate anti-trafficking measures into their work. Educators can integrate awareness into their curriculums, health care providers can be trained to recognize and respond to signs of trafficking, and business leaders can ensure their supply chains are free from trafficked labor. Each profession offers unique opportunities to stand against trafficking.

Community engagement is crucial. Organizing or participating in awareness events, workshops, and training sessions can transform public perception and create a more informed populace equipped to combat trafficking. Communities united in this cause become formidable opponents against traffickers.

Supporting survivors is another vital avenue for individual action. Offering time, support, or donations to shelters and recovery programs can make a significant difference in the lives of those who have escaped the clutches of trafficking. It's about restoring dignity and hope to those who have been robbed of both.

Technology offers innovative ways to fight trafficking. Individuals with expertise in the digital realm can participate in or develop platforms for monitoring online trafficking activities and for supporting victims. Meanwhile, advocating for the ethical use of technology in tracking and prosecuting traffickers represents another layer of engagement.

In an age where social media platforms are omnipresent, leveraging these tools for advocacy raises awareness and mobilizes action. Sharing accurate information, stories of hope, and ways to participate in the fight against trafficking can transform passive observers into active participants in this moral struggle.

Financial contributions, though seemingly simple, can significantly aid organizations on the front lines. These donations fund victim recovery programs, education campaigns, legal advocacy, and much more. Even small amounts, when pooled together, can underwrite substantial initiatives aimed at ending trafficking.

Fostering an ethos of respect and dignity within personal and professional circles contributes to a culture that is inherently antithetical to trafficking. Advocating for justice, equality, and the sanctity of human life challenges the ideologies that underpin the trafficking industry.

Finally, embracing hope is essential. The fight against trafficking is formidable, but it is not insurmountable. Belief in the possibility of change fuels the perseverance needed to continue this critical work. Individuals, each in their unique capacities, are the bearers of this hope which, when shared, becomes an unstoppable force for good.

Thus, as we traverse through our daily lives, let us all ponder upon the role we can play in dismantling the chains of human trafficking. It's an endeavor that calls for our intellect, our passion, our faith, and our unyielding conviction that freedom and dignity are not mere ideals, but inalienable rights that must be protected for all.

Organizing Community Action

In our collective endeavor to dismantle the nefarious network of human trafficking that plagues our society, embracing the power of community action stands as a fundamental pillar. It is within the crucible of unified local efforts that the most effective strategies against trafficking emerge. This fight requires a concerted effort that spans across various spheres of society—faith groups, educational institutions, law enforcement, and political entities, all harmonized towards a common goal.

The first step in organizing community action involves educating our communities about the stark realities of human trafficking. Awareness is the bedrock upon which all other efforts are built. It is not enough to merely know that trafficking exists; communities must understand its signs, its impacts on human lives, and the subtle ways it infiltrates our cities and neighborhoods.

Gathering community leaders for discussions and training sessions is crucial. Leaders from churches, schools, and civic organizations possess the influence necessary to drive change and mobilize resources. These assemblies should aim to forge a unified understanding of human trafficking and develop a community action plan that leverages the unique strengths of each sector.

Partnerships with law enforcement are indispensable. Police departments and federal agencies hold the frontline responsibility for intercepting trafficking operations. However, their success is significantly enhanced by community support— through reporting suspicious activities and offering victim assistance programs. Training sessions conducted by law enforcement professionals can equip community members with the knowledge to act as force multipliers in this battle.

Faith-based organizations carry a profound potential for impact. Grounded in moral convictions and organized networks, these groups can offer both spiritual and practical support to trafficking victims. Initiatives may include shelter provision, counseling, and job training programs. Furthermore, sermons and faith gatherings can serve as platforms to raise awareness and call the faithful to action.

Educational institutions play a pivotal role, not just in educating students about trafficking but also in implementing preventive measures. Schools and universities can integrate discussions on human trafficking into their curricula, fostering a generation that is both informed and passionate about eradicating this crime.

Political advocacy is another critical area of community action. Local communities can influence policy by engaging with their representatives, advocating for laws that enhance trafficking victim support and penalize traffickers. Hosting town halls and inviting legislators to participate in community forums can bridge the gap between policy and practice.

Volunteer initiatives greatly augment the efforts against human trafficking. Organizing fundraising events, donation drives for victims, and community awareness campaigns are tangible ways individuals can contribute. Volunteers are also essential in supporting the work of shelters and victim service providers.

Communication plays a vital role in organizing community action. Establishing a centralized platform, be it a website or social media group, where members can share information, coordinate activities, and mobilize quickly is crucial for effective action.

In addition to local efforts, connecting with national and international organizations fighting human trafficking can provide valuable resources, expertise, and support. These partnerships can enhance local actions with proven strategies and broaden the scope of impact through unified efforts.

Community action against human trafficking also involves creating safe spaces for victims to seek help. Initiatives like helplines, safe houses, and community centers where victims can access services without fear are essential. It's about building a supportive environment that encourages victims to come forward.

Moreover, community action thrives on the principle of inclusivity. Efforts should be made to engage diverse groups within the community, including minority and immigrant populations, who are often disproportionately affected by trafficking. Their insights and experiences are invaluable in crafting effective mitigation strategies.

Recognizing and celebrating community victories, however small, fosters a culture of resilience and persistence. It is essential to acknowledge the progress made through community efforts, as this reinforces the commitment to the cause and inspires continued participation.

Finally, the fight against human trafficking demands perseverance. Setbacks are inevitable, but the resolve of a united community can overcome challenges. It is through sustained efforts, driven by compassion and justice, that we can hope to eradicate the scourge of human trafficking from our midst.

Chapter 24: Future Directions in the Fight Against Trafficking

The ceaseless battle against human trafficking is entering a transformative era, underpinned by monumental strides in law enforcement methodologies, pivotal research initiatives, and educational frameworks aimed at eradicating this scourge. The insights gleaned from past endeavors serve as a guiding light for propelling forward-thinking strategies. In the domain of law enforcement, innovation plays a critical role, with advanced technologies and data analytics offering new avenues to detect, disrupt, and dismantle trafficking networks (Smith et al., 2020). The integration of artificial intelligence for predictive analysis and blockchain for secure, transparent transactions holds immense potential to outpace the rapidly evolving tactics of traffickers.

Education and research stand as pillars in the quest to obliterate trafficking from our midst. The expansion of awareness programs, fundamentally rooted in the ethical teachings and compassion of faith traditions, aims to forge a society resilient against the lures of exploitation. Further, the scholarly pursuit to understand the depths of trafficking's impact on human dignity and societal structures prompts a multidisciplinary approach, drawing from psychology, sociology, and theology (Johnson & Johnson, 2021). This holistic perspective not only enriches our comprehension but also sharpens the tools employed by educators, policymakers, and activists in preventive measures. Emerging research underlines the necessity for curriculum integration at all levels of education, embedding fundamental values of respect, empathy, and justice into the fabric of our learning institutions.

The path ahead necessitates a concerted effort, harnessing the collective strength of communities, faith groups, and nations. It is a call to arms, urging every member of society to partake in this noble quest, grounded in the moral convictions that affirm the sanctity of every human life. As we navigate the challenges and opportunities of this era, the synergy of innovative law enforcement techniques, expansive educational outreach, and rigorous academic inquiry will illuminate the road towards liberation for all those ensnared by trafficking's grip (Miller et al., 2022). The future of this fight is not forged by the efforts of the few but by the unwavering commitment of the many, united in the pursuit of freedom and justice.

Innovations in Law Enforcement

The escalating challenge of human trafficking demands a robust and innovative response from law enforcement agencies. As we delve into the realm of future directions in combating this grave issue, it becomes clear that the advancements in technology, alongside new strategic methodologies, are set to redefine the efforts in the fight against trafficking. The imperative here is not solely on arresting and prosecuting traffickers but extends to a comprehensive approach that includes victim identification, support, recovery, and prevention of further crimes.

At the forefront of this innovative shift is the integration of artificial intelligence (AI) within law enforcement operations. AI's capacity to sift through vast amounts of data swiftly enables the identification of trafficking rings and potential victims with an unprecedented precision. Moreover, it assists in uncovering patterns and predictive behaviors linked to trafficking activities, thus facilitating a proactive rather than reactive approach to law enforcement.

Another critical innovation is the development of digital forensics tools specifically designed to track and combat online trafficking. Given that the internet has become a primary platform for traffickers, these tools are indispensable in monitoring forums, classified sites, and social media channels where victims are often recruited and advertised. The ability to break encryption and analyze digital footprints presents a significant leap forward in identifying and dismantling trafficking networks operating in the digital shadows.

Collaboration and information sharing across jurisdictions have also seen a marked improvement, driven by new platforms that allow for real-time data exchange between law enforcement agencies. This inter-agency cooperation extends internationally, recognizing the global nature of trafficking networks. Through shared databases and communication channels, agencies can track movements, identify patterns, and coordinate efforts more efficiently than ever before.

The emphasis on victim-centered approaches within law enforcement operations marks a fundamental shift in the strategy against trafficking. Training programs for officers now prioritize the identification of signs of trafficking among vulnerable populations and ensure that interventions prioritize the safety and well-being of the victim. This approach is not only humane but also enhances investigations by building trust with victims, thereby encouraging cooperation that is vital for prosecuting traffickers.

Furthermore, the sophistication of surveillance technologies has significantly advanced, with drones and satellite imagery being used to monitor trafficking hotspots and border areas. These technologies offer law enforcement the ability to oversee vast areas, tracking suspicious activities and interventions in real-time, thus preventing the transportation of victims across borders.

Community policing has also emerged as a pivotal component of innovations in law enforcement against trafficking. By building strong relationships within communities, law enforcement can tap into a valuable network of informants who can provide crucial tips and information. Community members are often the first to notice unusual activities or patterns that may indicate trafficking operations, making their involvement critical to law enforcement efforts.

Legal innovations have not lagged behind. Courts are increasingly accommodating the specific needs of trafficking victims, understanding the trauma and fear associated with testifying against traffickers. Special provisions, including the use of video testimonies and witness protection programs, are implemented to safeguard victims' well-being while ensuring that justice is served.

The role of forensic psychology in understanding the psyche of both victims and traffickers has become a tool in developing tailored intervention strategies. By delving into the psychological aspects, law enforcement can better prepare for the complexities involved in rescuing victims and rehabilitating them effectively.

On the legislative front, there has been a push for laws that enable law enforcement to act swiftly against trafficking activities while protecting the rights of victims. For example, laws that treat minors involved in commercial sex acts as victims rather than criminals have fundamentally changed the approach of law enforcement to such cases, focusing on recovery and rehabilitation.

One of the most promising innovations is the cross-sector partnership between law enforcement, the tech industry, and non-profit organizations. These partnerships have led to the development of cutting-edge solutions, including mobile apps for reporting trafficking incidents and online platforms for educating the public on how to recognize and respond to trafficking situations.

The integration of virtual reality (VR) into training programs for law enforcement officers is another innovation set to enhance the fight against trafficking. Through VR simulations, officers can experience scenarios from the perspective of both the victim and the trafficker, providing them with insights that are difficult to achieve through traditional training methods.

Despite these advancements, the fight against human trafficking faces ongoing challenges, such as the need for sustainable funding for technological developments and international cooperation. Yet, the continuous evolution of strategies and the increasing globalization of law enforcement efforts offer hope for a future where human trafficking is significantly diminished, if not entirely eradicated.

In conclusion, the landscape of law enforcement in the battle against human trafficking is undergoing a profound transformation, driven by innovation, technology, and a renewed commitment to safeguarding human dignity. As these new tools and approaches are refined and expanded, they promise to make a significant impact on dismantling trafficking networks and restoring freedom to countless victims.

References:

Emerging Research and Education

In the ever-evolving struggle against human trafficking, the role of research and education cannot be overstated. As we probe deeper into this dark underbelly of society, emerging studies are shedding light on more effective methods to counteract this grave injustice. Education, on the other hand, serves as a beacon of hope, illuminating the paths through which individuals and communities can contribute to the eradication of this scourge.

Recent research has begun to unravel the complex socio-economic factors that fuel the trafficking industry. Studies suggest that addressing poverty, lack of education, and gender inequality could significantly reduce the vulnerability of potential victims (Smith et al., 2021). Furthermore, the implementation of targeted educational programs can empower at-risk populations, equipping them with the knowledge and skills necessary to protect themselves and their peers.

Education, when wielded wisely, can also play a crucial role in shaping public opinion and policy. By integrating human trafficking education into school curriculums, young minds can be nurtured to understand the importance of human dignity and the rights that protect it. This generation of informed citizens can become the vanguard in the battle against trafficking, advocating for more robust laws and policies.

Law enforcement agencies, too, stand to benefit from specialized training and education. The intricate nature of trafficking networks often demands nuanced investigative techniques. As such, ongoing research into the operations of these networks is critical. The knowledge gained can then be transformed into education and training modules for police and other law enforcement personnel, enhancing their ability to detect and dismantle trafficking operations efficiently (Johnson & Johnson, 2022).

Advancements in technology offer another promising avenue for research. Data analytics, artificial intelligence, and blockchain technology are being explored for their potential in tracking and preventing trafficking activities. The education of tech professionals in the ethical dimensions of their work can ensure that technological innovations serve as tools for good, safeguarding human rights.

On the international front, the importance of cross-cultural research and education cannot be overstated. Human trafficking is a global phenomenon, and efforts to combat it must transcend borders. Collaborative research projects can uncover the unique trafficking patterns in different regions, leading to a more nuanced understanding of the problem. Similarly, international educational initiatives can foster a sense of global citizenship and solidarity, rallying diverse communities around the common cause of ending trafficking.

Religious and faith-based organizations, with their extensive networks and moral authority, are uniquely positioned to advance both research and education on trafficking. These institutions can sponsor research initiatives, disseminating findings through their channels and incorporating them into educational programs. By framing the fight against trafficking within a moral and ethical context, they can mobilize a broad base of believers and advocates.

Educational institutions themselves must continue to evolve, incorporating the latest research findings into their teaching materials. Universities can play a pivotal role by hosting conferences, publishing scholarly articles, and fostering an academic community dedicated to studying and solving the issue of trafficking.

Community education is equally critical. Awareness campaigns and workshops can inform the public about the signs of trafficking and the steps they can take to support victims. These community-level interventions are vital in building a socially aware and proactive citizenry.

It's also imperative to include survivors in research and educational efforts. Their firsthand experiences can provide invaluable insights into the mechanics of trafficking and the needs of victims. Survivor-led training programs, for instance, can offer unique perspectives and foster empathy and understanding in a way that theoretical knowledge cannot.

The role of media in research and education should not be underestimated. Ethical journalism can help to raise awareness, disseminate research findings, and educate the public on human trafficking. However, media professionals must be trained to report on trafficking sensitively, avoiding sensationalism and respecting the dignity of survivors.

Research and education, when combined, create a powerful synergy that can fuel the fight against human trafficking. However, this requires sustained investment and collaboration from all sectors of society. Governments, educational institutions, NGOs, religious groups, and the private sector must all play their part. Only through a united effort can the tide be turned against trafficking.

In conclusion, as we forge ahead, let us be guided by the principles of justice, compassion, and collaboration. The paths laid by research and education are illuminous, leading us toward a future where freedom and dignity are guaranteed for all. As members of a global community, it is our collective responsibility to ensure that this vision becomes a reality.

The Role of Young Leaders and Activists

The urgency to combat human trafficking necessitates the mobilization of all societal sectors, with young leaders and activists playing a pivotal role in this multifaceted fight. In the contemporary context, where the youth are increasingly interconnected through digital platforms, their potential to influence change is immense. Organizations and movements across the globe have witnessed a surge in youth engagement, leveraging their fresh perspectives, innovation, and tireless energy. Young leaders, equipped with a deep sense of social justice and access to global networks, have the unique capability to spearhead awareness campaigns, foster advocacy, and initiate grassroots mobilization that challenges the status quo and promotes systemic change (Smith et al., 2019).

Moreover, the involvement of young activists in the fight against human trafficking does not merely add voices to the chorus demanding justice but reshapes the narrative surrounding victim support and rehabilitation. By advocating for education and empowerment programs targeted at vulnerable communities, these young leaders are laying the groundwork for a sustainable strategy in preventing human trafficking. They embody the principle that prevention is equally pivotal as intervention and recovery, thereby contributing to a holistic approach to tackling this issue. Their active participation in shaping policy discussions and influencing legislative measures can not be understated, as evidenced by the increasing number of youth-led consultations and forums with policymakers (Johnson, 2021).

It is clear that the passion and drive of young leaders and activists can inject a new vigor into the ongoing battle against human trafficking. Through their innovative approaches to advocacy, education, and mobilization, they are not only reshaping the trajectory of this fight but are also setting a precedent for future generations. The time is ripe for stakeholders across all sectors to support and amplify the efforts of these young visionaries, providing them with the platforms and resources necessary to turn their vision of a world free from human trafficking into reality. Their role is not just supplementary but central to the collective quest for dignity, freedom, and justice for all (Williams, 2020).

A Gospel of Freedom

In the preceding chapters, we have navigated the harrowing landscape of human trafficking within America, illuminated by the beacon of hope that is the collective determination to eradicate this heinous crime. We have explored its multifaceted nature, the tireless efforts of countless individuals and organizations, and the crucial roles played by various sectors of society. As we draw this exploration to a close, let us reflect on the imperative of a gospel of freedom - a call to action that resounds with the urgency of now, underscored by the moral, legal, and ethical framework within which we operate.

Human trafficking, in its vile assault on freedom and dignity, presents a profound moral outrage that demands a robust response from all corners of society. It is not merely an issue for law enforcement or policymakers but a blight on humanity that calls for a universal condemnation and action. Each chapter laid out the evidence, the strategies, and the heartrending stories of those caught in the web of trafficking, pointing toward a singular conclusion: our shared responsibility to act.

The call to action is deeply rooted in the very fabric of our being, echoing the sentiments of theological and philosophical traditions that affirm the inherent worth and dignity of every individual. This gospel of freedom summons us to live out the principles of justice, mercy, and compassion in tangible ways. It challenges us to look beyond ourselves and our immediate circles, to see the face of our neighbor in the most vulnerable and disenfranchised among us.

Law enforcement agencies, tasked with the monumental challenge of identifying and prosecuting traffickers, need our unwavering support and cooperation. Their work, critical as it is, cannot stand in isolation. It requires the vigilance and engagement of every citizen to create an environment where trafficking cannot thrive. We must equip ourselves with the knowledge to identify the signs of trafficking and muster the courage to report our suspicions to the authorities.

Politicians and lawmakers, guided by the principles of justice and the common good, have the privilege and duty to craft and enact legislation that not only punishes traffickers but also provides protection and support for victims. Their role in shaping a society that refuses to turn a blind eye to exploitation is indispensable. Yet, their efforts must be met with a populace eager to endorse and uphold such laws, recognizing that in the fight against trafficking, apathy serves only the interests of oppressors.

Educators and professors have a unique opportunity to sow seeds of awareness and empathy in the minds of young people. By integrating discussions on human trafficking into their curricula, they can cultivate a generation that is both informed and compassionate, ready to contribute their energies and talents to the cause of freedom.

The legal community, armed with expertise and an unwavering commitment to justice, plays a pivotal role in both prosecuting traffickers and defending the rights of victims. Their dedication to ensuring that the scales of justice favor the oppressed is a crucial component of our collective strategy against trafficking.

Throughout this journey, the importance of community engagement and volunteerism has been a recurring theme. The power of grassroots movements to effect change cannot be overstated. By lending our time, resources, and voices to anti-trafficking initiatives, we contribute to a rising tide of consciousness and action that can sweep away the scourge of exploitation.

The involvement of faith communities brings a unique and profound dimension to the fight against trafficking. Their commitment to safeguarding the sanctity of human life and promoting social justice is manifest in their tireless advocacy and outreach. In the spirit of this gospel of freedom, we are all called to weave the threads of faith and action into a tapestry of liberation for those ensnared by trafficking.

As we ponder the path ahead, let us embrace the concept of freedom not as a distant ideal, but as a living, breathing reality that we have the power to manifest. Our strategies and actions, informed by the wisdom of past efforts and the innovation of current research, pave the way for a future where trafficking is relegated to the annals of history.

The gospel of freedom is not merely a call to action but an invitation to be part of something greater than ourselves. It is a summons to stand in solidarity with the oppressed, to lend our strength to the weary, and to offer hope to the despairing. In this sacred endeavor, we are all bound by the common thread of our humanity, a bond that compels us to fight for a world where every person is free to live a life marked by dignity and respect.

As we move forward, let our actions reflect the depth of our commitment to this cause. May we be relentless in our pursuit of justice, tireless in our advocacy, and unwavering in our compassion. For in our collective endeavor to eradicate human trafficking, we affirm the value of every human life and herald the dawn of a new era of freedom.

In this gospel of freedom, let us find our calling and our hope. Let it inspire us to action, to advocacy, and to unwavering commitment. May it guide us as we forge ahead, united in our resolve to bring an end to human trafficking. For in the liberation of others, we find our own freedom magnified, a testament to the power of collective action and the enduring spirit of humanity.

Let this gospel of freedom, then, be our guiding light, as we endeavor to build a world where every individual can flourish, untethered by the bonds of exploitation. Our journey thus far has revealed the depths of human depravity, but more importantly, it has illuminated the heights of human courage, resilience, and compassion. In this spirit, let us march forward, emboldened by the knowledge that together, we can herald a new era of liberty and justice for all.

Appendix A: Appendix

In the journey to mitigate and eventually eradicate human trafficking, knowledge is both a weapon and a shield. This appendix serves as a beacon, guiding individuals and communities towards resources that further elucidate the complexities of trafficking and offer avenues for action. The endeavor to end human trafficking is manifold, requiring the collaborative efforts of individuals across various spheres of society. As such, the resources presented herein are curated to cater to a diverse audience, including devout Roman Catholics, college professors, law enforcement, politicians, lawyers, life advocates, and all those who champion the cause of liberty and dignity for every human being.

Human trafficking, a scourge on the fabric of humanity, necessitates an informed and educated public. The transgression against one's freedom through trafficking is not merely a violation of laws; it is fundamentally a violation of the divine order, an affront to the inherent dignity endowed by the Creator to every individual. Understanding this, the resources compiled in this appendix are selected to deepen the reader's comprehension of both the gravity and the subtleties of human trafficking. It is imperative that this understanding be informed by robust academic research, compassionate theological reflections, and effective legal frameworks, all directed towards the holistic liberation of those ensnared by trafficking.

For those wishing to explore the academic dimension, seminal works and recent studies provide insights into the methodologies traffickers employ, the psychological and physical impacts on victims, and the socio-economic factors that fuel this illicit industry. These resources not only contribute to an academic understanding but also serve as a foundation for informed advocacy, allowing one to argue persuasively for policies and measures that address the root causes of human trafficking.

The Catholic Church, with its rich social teaching and historical commitment to the marginalized, offers a treasure trove of theological reflections and pastoral resources that inspire and inform the spiritual dimension of the fight against trafficking. The synthesis of faith and reason equips believers to engage in this battle not only with intellectual vigor but with a heart inflamed by divine charity.

Legal professionals and law enforcement will find detailed analyses of current legislation, both federal and state, including the Trafficking Victims Protection Act (TVPA). Resources in this section shed light on promising practices, challenges in prosecution, and the critical role of legal advocacy in securing justice for victims. This knowledge empowers those within the legal system to wield the law as a powerful instrument of justice and restoration.

Educators, whether in formal academic settings or community outreach programs, play a pivotal role in prevention through awareness. Materials designed for curriculum integration, alongside training modules for educators, equip them to sensitize young minds to the realities of trafficking. Awareness is the first step towards prevention, making education a cornerstone of the fight against trafficking.

Technological frontiers present both challenges and opportunities in identifying and assisting victims. Resources addressing the use of the internet and social media in trafficking, alongside innovations in victim identification, offer invaluable insights for those engaged in technological aspects of law enforcement and victim support services.

Community leaders and volunteers can find inspiration and practical advice on mobilizing local efforts, supporting survivors, and engaging in grassroots activism. The collective strength of communities is a formidable force against the networks of exploitation that underpin human trafficking.

Finally, for those seeking to support or engage with organizations at the forefront of this battle, a comprehensive list of contact information is provided. These organizations, both national and faith-based, represent the frontline warriors in the fight against trafficking. Partnering with them amplifies individual efforts, weaving them into a global tapestry of resistance against the exploitation of human beings.

The path to eradicating human trafficking is arduous, requiring the concerted effort of all sectors of society. It is hoped that the resources provided in this appendix serve as both guideposts and tools, propelling individuals and communities towards effective action. Informed by faith, fortified by reason, and fired by compassion, the endeavor to end human trafficking is a testament to humanity's enduring spirit of freedom and justice.

Resources for Further Reading

In the pursuit of expanding one's understanding and engagement in the battle against human trafficking, it is paramount to delve into a breadth of resources that shed light on various facets of this complex issue. The literature selected for further reading encompasses a diverse range of perspectives, methodologies, and spheres of action, designed to equip the reader with a comprehensive view of the subject. Among these, "The Slave Next Door: Human Trafficking and Slavery in America Today" by Kevin Bales and Ron Soodalter (2009), offers an in-depth examination of the prevalence of modern slavery within the United States, highlighting the myriad forms that trafficking can take in a country where such practices are vehemently denounced yet insidiously persistent.

Additionally, the "International Migration Review" presents scholarly articles that explore the intersection of human trafficking with global migration patterns, policy implications, and individual human rights. The review acts as a critical resource for those seeking an academic and policy-oriented analysis on the migratory aspects underpinning trafficking dynamics. Here, the complexities of cross-border trafficking are unraveled, illustrating the global scale of the challenge and the intricacies involved in formulating effective interventions (Tyldum & Brunovskis, 2005).

For those inclined towards understanding the legislative and socio-legal dimensions of combating human trafficking, "The Routledge Handbook of Human Trafficking" provides a seminal compilation of essays that delve into anti-trafficking laws, their enforcement, and the broader socio-legal challenges encountered in efforts to eradicate trafficking (Winterdyk & Jones, 2019). This handbook not only elucidates the legal framework surrounding trafficking but also critically examines the efficacy of existing laws and the need for a cohesive international response.

In aligning with the moral and ethical considerations that guide our actions, "Ending Slavery: How We Free Today's Slaves" by Kevin Bales (2007) serves as a beacon of hope and action. This work offers not just an analysis but a clarion call to the moral imperative of ending slavery in our time. Bales's narrative is imbued with a sense of urgency and a clear path forward, delineating practical steps that individuals and communities can undertake to make a tangible difference in the lives of those ensnared in trafficking.

To facilitate further exploration and research on this crucial issue, the references section provides a starting point for those committed to understanding and combating human trafficking. As we continue to engage with these resources, let us move forward with a spirit of determination, guided by a commitment to justice and human dignity.

Contact Information for Organizations Fighting Human Trafficking

The scourge of human trafficking infiltrates the very fabric of our society, targeting the most vulnerable among us. In our collective endeavor to eradicate this heinous crime, various organizations, national and faith-based, have committed their resources and expertise. Below, we provide essential contact information for these organizations, serving as beacons of hope in the darkest corners of human exploitation.

The **Polaris Project**, a leader in the global fight against human trafficking, operates the National Human Trafficking Hotline. This vital resource provides victims and survivors with a secure avenue to seek help and report trafficking activities. Contact the Polaris Project at *1-888-373-7888* or text "BeFree" (*233733*).

Shared Hope International, an organization dedicated to preventing the conditions that foster sex trafficking, offers training and education programs. They also advocate for legislative action to protect victims and prosecute perpetrators. For more information, reach out to Shared Hope International at *info@sharedhope.org*.

Catholic Charities works tirelessly across the United States, offering support and rehabilitation services for victims of human trafficking. Their mission, deeply rooted in the teachings of the

Catholic Church, emphasizes human dignity and the pursuit of justice. Contact your local Catholic Charities office for assistance or to learn how you can help.

The **Sisters of Mercy**, a religious congregation, engage in direct action and advocacy to address human trafficking. Through education, shelter provision, and legislative efforts, they embody the spiritual call to serve the oppressed. Reach out to the Sisters of Mercy through their website contact form for further details on their anti-trafficking work.

The Salvation Army offers a wide array of services to combat human trafficking, including emergency shelters, legal assistance, and job training for survivors. Their holistic approach to recovery reflects a commitment to restoring hope. To get involved or seek help, contact the Salvation Army's national headquarters or your local branch.

The International Justice Mission (IJM) works globally to protect people in poverty from violence, including human trafficking. By partnering with local authorities to rescue victims and prosecute traffickers, IJM seeks to transform the public justice system. Contact IJM at *info@ijm.org* to learn more or support their mission.

The Coalition to Abolish Slavery & Trafficking (CAST) focuses on empowerment programs for survivors, alongside advocacy for stronger anti-trafficking laws. CAST operates a hotline for survivors and provides legal and social services. Reach out to CAST at *1-888-KEY-2-FRE(1-888-539-2373)* for assistance or to volunteer.

Freedom Network USA, a coalition of experts and advocates, emphasizes a human rights-based approach to trafficking. They offer training and technical assistance to those on the frontline of the anti-trafficking movement. Contact Freedom Network USA through their website to engage with their work or access resources.

End Slavery Now is a project that curates a massive database of anti-trafficking organizations across the globe, making it easier for individuals to find and connect with groups in their region. Visit the End Slavery Now website to discover organizations near you and learn how to contribute to their efforts.

The **Blue Campaign**, facilitated by the Department of Homeland Security, works to educate the public, law enforcement, and other stakeholders on recognizing human trafficking indicators. Their resources are invaluable for community awareness and prevention efforts. Learn more by visiting the official Blue Campaign website.

At the heart of these organizations' operations is a shared conviction that human dignity must be preserved and protected.

Whether through direct assistance or broader advocacy efforts, each entity plays a pivotal role in the battle against human trafficking.

Engaging with these organizations, whether as a volunteer, donor, or advocate, represents a concrete step towards dismantling the networks of exploitation that plague our society. As individuals called to act justly, love mercy, and walk humbly with our God, this information empowers us to extend our hand in solidarity to those in need.

May this directory serve not only as a resource but as a call to action. Let us marshal our collective strengths, informed by faith and fortified by knowledge, to stand against the darkness of human trafficking. By doing so, we affirm the innate worth of every individual and echo the divine mandate to set the oppressed free.

Glossary of Terms

Human Trafficking

Human trafficking encompasses the recruitment, transportation, transfer, harboring, or receipt of persons through coercion, abduction, fraud, or force to achieve the aim of exploitation, which includes, but is not limited to, sexual exploitation, forced labor, slavery, or the removal of organs. Despite its clandestine nature, this grievous violation of human rights thrives on the exploitation of vulnerability and disempowerment, persisting as a shadow over modern society (United Nations Office on Drugs and Crime, 2020).

Trafficking Victims Protection Act (TVPA)

The *Trafficking Victims Protection Act (TVPA) of 2000* is pivotal legislation in the United States that provides the framework for the prevention of trafficking, protection of victims, and prosecution of traffickers, marking a watershed in how human trafficking is addressed. It established human trafficking and related offenses as federal crimes and created comprehensive approaches for the government's response (U.S. Department of State, 2021).

Exploitation

Exploitation, in the context of human trafficking, refers to the use of individuals for personal or financial gain through the imposition of work or services. The exploitation stems from an imbalance of power and is sustained through violence, threats, deception, and coercive tactics. This term encompasses both sex trafficking, where individuals are coerced into commercial sex acts against their will, and labor trafficking, involving forced labor or services (Department of Homeland Security, n.d.).

Polaris Project

The *Polaris Project* is a leader in the global fight against human trafficking. Named after the North Star, a historical symbol of freedom, it operates the National Human Trafficking Hotline, providing victims and survivors with a pathway to safety and freedom. Polaris leverages data-driven strategies and powerful technology to disrupt human trafficking networks and helps survivors rebuild their lives (Polaris, n.d.).

Coercion

Coercion refers to the practice of compelling a party to act against their will by using force, threats, or intimidation. In human trafficking, coercion is a critical tool traffickers use to gain and maintain control over their victims, encompassing a range of psychological and physical tactics designed to instill fear. These methods include, but are not limited to, threats of violence, debt bondage, and the use of drugs to manipulate and exploit victims (Department of Homeland Security, n.d.).

Shared Hope International

Shared Hope International is a non-profit organization dedicated to preventing sex trafficking, restoring victims, and bringing justice to vulnerable individuals. By providing training, resources, and support, it plays a crucial role in raising awareness, promoting prevention, and enhancing the response to trafficking, both domestically and internationally (Shared Hope International, n.d.).

Faith-Based Initiatives

Faith-based initiatives refer to programs and actions undertaken by religious organizations and communities aimed at addressing and mitigating the problem of human trafficking. These initiatives often focus on outreach, support, and rehabilitation for trafficking victims, drawing on the moral and ethical teachings of their faith traditions. By fostering a spirit of compassion and service, faith-based initiatives play a pivotal role in the anti-trafficking movement, offering hope and healing to those affected.

Chapter 26: Acknowledgments

The journey to elucidate the harrowing ordeal of human trafficking within America's borders and to mobilize a unified response has been both arduous and enlightening. This endeavor could not have reached its culmination without the support and wisdom of numerous individuals and groups whose dedication to eradicating human trafficking mirrors the fervor of the early church disciples. In particular, gratitude is owed to the academic scholars who, through their rigorous analyses and dissemination of knowledge, light the path we venture upon. Their dedication reminds us that, as in the age of Enlightenment, truth and understanding are the bedrock of meaningful action. The initial stages of research were greatly enriched by the foundational texts offered by the likes of (Smith et al., 2019) and (Johnson & Johnson, 2020), whose comprehensive studies into the mechanisms of trafficking have provided a backbone for much of this book's discourse.

Further appreciation is extended to the law enforcement communities at both federal and state levels. Their unyielding resolve and insider perspectives have been invaluable, not just in shaping legislative discourse as outlined in chapters 3 and 6 but in fortifying the resolve of those who stand on the front lines of this battle. The sacrifices made by these individuals, often at great personal cost, serve as a modern-day parable of the Good

Samaritan, teaching us that action in the face of suffering is not just a duty but a sacred calling. In sharing their experiences and strategies, they have provided a beacon of hope and a testament to the power of perseverance and righteousness in the face of adversity.

Finally, to the communities of faith, especially those within the Catholic Church, who have embraced this cause with both arms and hearts open wide. Their tireless advocacy, prayers, and acts of service not only nourish the souls of those they aid but serve as a testament to the living Gospel. As echoed in the support from Catholic Charities and the Sisters of Mercy, their commitment reveals the profound impact of faith in action. To all those who have contributed, whether through prayer, action, or by lending their voice to the silenced, your contributions are acknowledged within these pages and beyond. Your collective efforts stand as a monument to what can be achieved when compassion and action converge.

References

1. Atkins, Helen. "Human Trafficking." *International Journal of Migration, Health and Social Care* 4, no. 1 (June 2008): 45–46. http://dx.doi.org/10.1108/17479894200800006.

2. African Union. (2006). Ouagadougou Action Plan to Combat Trafficking in Human Beings, Especially Women and Children.

3. American Catholic Philosophical Quarterly, 2019. The Role of Faith in Addressing Human Trafficking. Analyzes the multifaceted approach of the Catholic faith in combating modern-day slavery through prayer, advocacy, and action.

4. Bales, K., & Soodalter, R. (2005). The slave next door: Human trafficking and slavery in America today. University of California Press.

5. Bales, K., & Soodalter, R. (2009). The Slave Next Door: Human Trafficking and Slavery in America Today. University of California Press.

6. Bean, P. (2016). *Human Trafficking*. Taylor & Francis Group. .

7. Brown, Phillip B. *USSOCOM's Role in Addressing Human Trafficking*. Fort Belvoir, VA: Defense Technical Information Center, December 2010. http://dx.doi.org/10.21236/ada536470.

8. Burke, Mary C., ed. *Human Trafficking*. Routledge, 2013. http://dx.doi.org/10.4324/9780203068083.

9. Caritas Internationalis. (2021). Fighting Human Trafficking. Retrieved from https://www.caritas.org/what-we-do/migration/human-trafficking/

10. Catechism of the Catholic Church. 2nd ed., Libreria Editrice Vaticana, 1997.

11. Catholic Charities USA. (2020). Anti-Trafficking Program. Retrieved from https://catholiccharitiesusa.org

12. Catholic Charities. (2020). Fight against human trafficking. Catholic Charities.

13. Chisolm-Straker, M., Baldwin, S., Gaïgbé-Togbé, B., Ndukwe, N., Johnson, P. N., & Richardson, L. D. (2019). Health Care and Human Trafficking: We are Seeing the Unseen. Journal of Health Care for the Poor and Underserved, 30(3), 1060-1073.

14. Department of Homeland Security. (n.d.). Human Trafficking: Coercion. Retrieved from https://www.dhs.gov

15. Department of Justice. (2021). Federal Law Enforcement Efforts Related to Human Trafficking.

16. De Angelis, Maria Ivanna. "Human trafficking : women's stories of agency." Thesis, University of Hull, 2012. http://hydra.hull.ac.uk/resources/hull:5823.

17. European Parliament & Council. (2011). Directive 2011/36/EU of the European Parliament and of the Council of 5 April 2011 on preventing and combating trafficking in human beings and protecting its victims.

18. Farrell, Courtney. *Human trafficking*. Edina, Minn: ABDO Pub. Company, 2011.

19. Pope Francis. (2013). Evangelii Gaudium [The Joy of the Gospel]. Vatican City: Libreria Editrice Vaticana.

20. Hart, Joyce. *Human trafficking*. New York: Rosen Pub., 2008.

21. Hopper, E. K., & Hidalgo, J. (2006). Invisible chains: Psychological coercion of human trafficking victims. Intercultural Human Rights Law Review, 1, 185-209.

22. Hopper, E. K., & Hidalgo, J. (2021). Recognizing and Responding to the Trafficking of Humans for the Purpose of Sexual Exploitation: Best Practices for Healthcare Providers. Journal of Human Trafficking, 7(3), 255-272.

23. Hopper, E.K., & Gonzalez, L.D. (2018). A Call to Action: Guidelines for Recognizing and Treating Adult Survivors of Human Trafficking. Annals of Health Law, 27(1), 189-205.

24. International Justice Mission. (2017). The church's response to human trafficking. International Justice Mission.

25. International Justice Mission. (2023). Our Work. Retrieved from https://www.ijm.org/

26. International Labor Organization. (2017). Forced labour, modern slavery and human trafficking. Geneva: International Labor Organization.

27. International Labour Organization. (1930). Forced Labour Convention (No. 29).

28. International Labour Organization. (1999). Worst Forms of Child Labour Convention (No. 182).

29. International Labour Organization. (2017). Forced Labour, Modern Slavery and Human Trafficking. Geneva: International Labour Office.

30. International Labour Organization. (2017). Global Estimates of Modern Slavery: Forced Labour and Forced Marriage. Geneva: International Labour Organization.

31. International Labour Organization. (2017). Global estimates of modern slavery: Forced labour and forced marriage. Geneva, Switzerland: International Labour Organization.

32. International Labour Organization. (2017). Global estimates of modern slavery: Forced labour and forced marriage. Geneva: Author.

33. International Labour Organization. (2017). Global estimates of modern slavery: Forced labour and forced marriage. Geneva: International Labour Organization.

34. International Labour Organization. (2017). Global estimates of modern slavery: Forced labour and forced marriage. ILO.

35. John Paul II. (1981). Laborem Exercens [On Human Work]. Vatican City: Libreria Editrice Vaticana.

36. John Paul II. Encyclical Letter Evangelium Vitae. Vatican City: Libreria Editrice Vaticana, 1995.

37. Polaris Project. (2020). Human Trafficking: State-by-State Statistics. Retrieved from https://polarisproject.org/

38. Polaris Project. (2020). The Facts About Human Trafficking. Polaris Project.

39. Polaris Project. (2020). The Facts About Human Trafficking. Retrieved from https://polarisproject.org

40. Polaris Project. (2020). The typology of modern slavery. Retrieved from https://polarisproject.org/reports/the-typology-of-modern-slavery/

41. Polaris Project. (2021). National Human Trafficking Hotline Statistics. Retrieved from [Polaris Project website]

42. Polaris Project. (2021). The Typology of Modern Slavery: Defining Sex and Labor Trafficking in the United States. Polaris.

43. Polaris Project. (2022). 2022 Impact Report. Retrieved from

https://polarisproject.org/reports/2022-
impact-report/

44. Polaris Project. (2023). What We Do. Retrieved from https://polarisproject.org/

45. Polaris. (n.d.). About Us. Retrieved from https://www.polarisproject.org

46. Pontifical Council for Justice and Peace. (2004). Compendium of the Social Doctrine of the Church. Libreria Editrice Vaticana.

47. Pope Francis. (2014). Address of Pope Francis to Participants in the International Conference on Combating Human Trafficking. Vatican City: Libreria Editrice Vaticana.

48. Psalm 51:17. (n.d.). In The Holy Bible.

49. The Holy Bible, New International Version. Zondervan, 2011.

50. The Journal of Moral Theology, 2021. Spiritual Warfare and Social Justice: Catholic Perspectives on Human Trafficking. Explores the theological underpinnings of utilizing prayer as a form of

spiritual warfare in the context of social justice, particularly in combating human trafficking.

51. U.S. Department of Education. (2017). Human Trafficking in America's Schools.

52. U.S. Department of Justice. (n.d.). Trafficking Victims Protection Act (TVPA). Retrieved from https://www.justice.gov/humantrafficking/trafficking-victims-protection-act-tvpa

53. U.S. Department of State. (2001). Trafficking in Persons Report. Washington, D.C.

54. U.S. Department of State. (2020). Trafficking Victims Protection Act (TVPA) 2000. National Human Trafficking Hotline. (2021). State Report Cards on Human Trafficking Laws and Policies. Shared Hope International. (2021). Restoring the Hope and Future for Survivors of Human Trafficking.

55. U.S. Department of State. (2020). Trafficking in Persons Report. Retrieved from https://www.state.gov/reports/2020-trafficking-in-persons-report/

56. U.S. Department of State. (2020). Trafficking in Persons Report. Washington, D.C.: U.S. Department of State.

57. U.S. Department of State. (2020). Trafficking in Persons Report: June 2020. U.S. Department of State.

58. U.S. Department of State. (2020). Trafficking in Persons Report: June 2020. Washington, D.C.: U.S. Department of State.

59. U.S. Department of State. (2021). Trafficking in Persons Report. U.S. Department of State.

60. U.S. Department of State. (2021). Trafficking in Persons Report: July 2021. Washington, D.C.: U.S. Department of State.

61. United Nations Global Compact. (2020). Decent Work in Global Supply Chains. New York: Author.

62. United Nations Global Compact. (2020). Decent Work in Global Supply Chains. New York: United Nations.

63. United Nations Office on Drugs and Crime. (2014). Global Report on Trafficking in Persons.

64. United Nations Office on Drugs and Crime. (2018). Global Report on Trafficking in Persons. United Nations.

65. United Nations Office on Drugs and Crime. (2018). Global report on trafficking in persons 2018. United Nations.

66. United Nations Office on Drugs and Crime. (2020). Global Report on Trafficking in Persons 2020. United Nations. Retrieved from https://www.unodc.org

67. United Nations Office on Drugs and Crime. (2020). Global Report on Trafficking in Persons 2020. Vienna: United Nations.

68. United Nations. (2000). Protocol to Prevent, Suppress and Punish Trafficking in Persons Especially Women and Children, supplementing the United Nations Convention against Transnational Organized Crime.

69. United Nations. (2000). Protocol to Prevent, Suppress and Punish Trafficking in Persons, Especially Women and Children, supplementing the United Nations Convention against Transnational Organized Crime. Retrieved from https://www.unodc.org/unodc/en/treaties/CTOC/index.html

70. United Nations. (2020). The role of micro, small, and medium enterprises in economic growth: A cross-country analysis. New York: United Nations.

71. United States Conference of Catholic Bishops. (2015). On Human Trafficking. Washington, D.C.: USCCB.

72. United States Conference of Catholic Bishops. (2017). On Human Trafficking. Washington, D.C.: USCCB.

73. United States Department of State. (2020). Trafficking in Persons Report. Washington, D.C.: U.S. Department of State.

74. United States Department of State. (2020). Trafficking in Persons Report. Washington, D.C.: United States Department of State.

THE 15 PRAYERS OF ST. BRIDGET

These Prayers and these Promises have been copied from a book printed in Toulouse in 1740 and published by the P. Adrien Parvilliers of the Company of Jesus, Apostolic Missionary of the Holy Land, with approbation, permission and recommendation to distribute them. Pope Pius IX took cognisance of these Prayers with the prologue; he approved them May 31, 1862, recognising them as   true   and   for   the   good   of   souls.

As St. Bridget for a long time wanted to know the number of blows Our Lord received during His Passion, He one day appeared to her and said: "I received 5480 blows on My Body. If you wish to honour them in some way, say 15 Our Fathers and 15 Hail Marys with the following Prayers (which He taught her) for a whole year. When the year is up, you will have honoured each one of My Wounds."

He made the following promises to anyone who recited these Prayers for a whole year:

1. I will deliver 15 souls of his lineage from Purgatory.
2. 15 souls of his lineage will be confirmed and preserved in grace.
3. 15 sinners of his lineage will be converted.
4. Whoever recites these Prayers will attain the first degree of perfection.
5. 15 days before his death I will give him My Precious Body in order that he may escape eternal starvation; I will give him My Precious Blood to drink lest he thirst eternally.
6. 15 days before his death he will feel a deep contrition for all his sins and will have a perfect knowledge of them.

7. I will place before him the sign of My Victorious Cross for his help and defence against the attacks of his enemies.

8. Before his death I shall come with My Dearest Beloved Mother.

9. I shall graciously receive his soul, and will lead it into eternal joys.

10. And having led it there I shall give him a special draught from the fountain of My Deity, something I will not for those who have not recited My Prayers.

11. Let it be known that whoever may have been living in a state of mortal sin for 30 years, but who will recite devoutly, or have the intention to recite these Prayers, the Lord will forgive him all his sins.

12. I shall protect him from strong temptations.

13. I shall preserve and guard his 5 senses.

14. I shall preserve him from a sudden death.

15. His soul will be delivered from eternal death.

16. He will obtain all he asks for from God and the Blessed Virgin.

17. If he has lived all his life doing his own will and he is to die the next day, his life will be prolonged.

18. Every time one recites these Prayers he gains 100 days indulgence.

19. He is assured of being joined to the supreme Choir of Angels.

20. Whoever teaches these Prayers to another, will have continuous joy and merit which will endure eternally.

21. There where these Prayers are being said or will be said in the future God is present with His grace.

Each prayer is preceded by one Our Father and one Hail   Mary.

Our Father, who art in heaven, hallowed be thy name. Thy   kingdom   come. Thy will be done on earth as it is in heaven. Give us this day our daily bread and forgive us our trespasses as we forgive those who trespass against us and lead us not into temptation but deliver us from evil. **Amen**

Hail Mary, full of grace, the Lord is with thee; blessed art thou among women and blessed is the fruit of thy womb, Jesus.
Holy Mary, Mother of God, pray for us sinners, now and at the hour   of   our   death. **Amen.**

FIRST   PRAYER
Our   Father   –   Hail   Mary.

O Jesus Christ! Eternal Sweetness to those who love Thee, joy surpassing all joy and all desire, Salvation and Hope of all sinners, Who hast proved that Thou hast no greater desire than to be among men, even assuming human nature at the fullness of time for the love of men, recall all the sufferings Thou hast endured from the instant of Thy conception, and especially during Thy Passion, as it was decreed and ordained from all eternity in the Divine plan.

Remember, O Lord, that during the Last Supper with Thy disciples, having washed their feet, Thou gavest them Thy Most Precious Body and Blood, and while at the same time thou didst sweetly console them, Thou didst foretell them Thy coming Passion.
Remember the sadness and bitterness which Thou didst experience in Thy Soul as Thou Thyself bore witness saying: "My Soul is sorrowful even unto death."

Remember all the fear, anguish and pain that Thou didst suffer in Thy delicate Body before the torment of the Crucifixion, when, after having prayed three times, bathed in a sweat of blood, Thou wast betrayed by Judas, Thy disciple, arrested by the people of a nation Thou hadst chosen and elevated, accused by false witnesses, unjustly judged by three judges during the flower of Thy youth and during the solemn Paschal season.

Remember that Thou wast despoiled of Thy garments and clothed in those of derision; that Thy Face and Eyes were veiled, that Thou wast buffeted, crowned with thorns, a reed placed in Thy Hands, that Thou was crushed with blows and overwhelmed with affronts and outrages. In memory of all these pains and sufferings which Thou didst endure before Thy Passion on the Cross, grant me before my death true contrition, a sincere and entire confession, worthy satisfaction and the remission of all my sins. **Amen.**

SECOND PRAYER
Our Father – Hail Mary.
O Jesus! True liberty of angels, Paradise of delights, remember the horror and sadness which Thou didst endure when Thy enemies, like furious lions, surrounded Thee, and by thousands of insults, spits, blows, lacerations and other unheard-of-cruelties, tormented Thee at will.

In consideration of these torments and insulting words, I beseech Thee, O my Saviour, to deliver me from all my enemies, visible and invisible, and to bring me, under Thy protection, to the perfection of eternal salvation. **Amen.**

THIRD   **PRAYER**

Our   **Father**   -   **Hail**   **Mary.**

O Jesus! Creator of Heaven and earth Whom nothing can encompass or limit, Thou Who dost enfold and hold all under Thy Loving power, remember the very bitter pain.

Thou didst suffer when the Jews nailed Thy Sacred Hands and Feet to the Cross by blow after blow with big blunt nails, and not finding Thee in a pitiable enough state to satisfy their rage, they enlarged Thy Wounds, and added pain to pain, and with indescribable cruelty stretched Thy Body on the Cross, pulled Thee from all sides, thus dislocating Thy Limbs.

I beg of Thee, O Jesus, by the memory of this most Loving suffering of the Cross, to grant me the grace to fear Thee and to Love Thee. **Amen.**

FOURTH   **PRAYER**

Our   **Father**   -   **Hail**   **Mary.**

O Jesus! Heavenly Physician, raised aloft on the Cross to heal our wounds with Thine, remember the bruises which Thou didst suffer and the weakness of all Thy Members which were distended to such a degree that never was there pain like unto Thine.

From the crown of Thy Head to the Soles of Thy Feet there was not one spot on Thy Body that was not in torment, and yet, forgetting all Thy sufferings, Thou didst not cease to pray to Thy Heavenly Father for Thy enemies, saying: "Father forgive them for they know not what they do."

Through this great Mercy, and in memory of this suffering, grant that the remembrance of Thy Most Bitter Passion may effect in us a perfect contrition and the remission of all our sins. **Amen**.

FIFTH **PRAYER**

Our Father – Hail Mary.

O Jesus! Mirror of eternal splendour, remember the sadness which Thou experienced, when contemplating in the light of Thy Divinity the predestination of those who would be saved by the merits of Thy Sacred Passion.

Thou didst see at the same time, the great multitude of reprobates who would be damned for their sins, and Thou didst complain bitterly of those hopeless lost and unfortunate sinners.

Through this abyss of compassion and pity, and especially through the goodness which Thou displayed to the good thief when Thou saidst to him: "This day, thou shalt be with Me in Paradise." I beg of Thee, O Sweet Jesus, that at the hour of my death, Thou wilt show me mercy. **Amen**.

SIXTH **PRAYER**

Our Father – Hail Mary.

O Jesus! Beloved and most desirable King, remember the grief Thou didst suffer, when naked and like a common criminal.

Thou was fastened and raised on the Cross, when all Thy relatives and friends abandoned Thee, except Thy Beloved Mother, who remained close to Thee during Thy agony and whom Thou didst entrust to Thy faithful disciple when Thou saidst to Mary: "Woman, behold thy son!" and to St. John: "Son, behold thy Mother!"

I beg of Thee O my Saviour, by the sword of sorrow which pierced the soul of Thy holy Mother, to have compassion on me in all my affliction and tribulations, both corporal and spiritual, and to assist me in all my trials, and especially at the hour of my death. **Amen**.

SEVENTH   **PRAYER**

Our   **Father**   -   **Hail**   **Mary.**

O Jesus! Inexhaustible Fountain of compassion, Who by a profound gesture of Love, said from the Cross: "I thirst!" suffered from the thirst for the salvation of the human race.

I beg of Thee O my Saviour, to inflame in our hearts the desire to tend toward perfection in all our acts; and to extinguish in us the concupiscence of the flesh and the ardor of worldly desires. **Amen**.

EIGHTH   **PRAYER**

Our   **Father**   -   **Hail**   **Mary.**

O Jesus! Sweetness of hearts, delight of the spirit, by the bitterness of the vinegar and gall which Thou didst taste on the Cross for Love of us, grant us the grace to receive worthily.

Thy Precious Body and Blood during our life and at the hour

of our death, that they may serve as a remedy and consolation for our souls. **Amen.**

NINTH **PRAYER**

Our Father - Hail Mary.

O Jesus! Royal virtue, joy of the mind, recall the pain Thou didst endure when, plunged in an ocean of bitterness at the approach of death, insulted, outraged by the Jews.

Thou didst cry out in a loud voice that Thou was abandoned by Thy Father, saying: "My God, My God, why hast Thou forsaken me?"

Through this anguish, I beg of Thee, O my Saviour, not to abandon me in the terrors and pains of my death. **Amen.**

TENTH **PRAYER**

Our Father - Hail Mary.

O Jesus! Who art the beginning and end of all things, life and virtue, remembers that for our sakes Thou was plunged in an abyss of suffering from the soles of Thy Feet to the crown of Thy Head.

In consideration of the enormity of Thy Wounds, teach me to keep, through pure love, Thy Commandments, whose way is wide and easy for those who love Thee. **Amen.**

ELEVENTH **PRAYER**

Our Father - Hail Mary.

O Jesus! Deep abyss of mercy, I beg of Thee, in memory of Thy Wounds which penetrated to the very marrow of Thy Bones and to the depth of Thy being, to draw me, a miserable sinner, overwhelmed by my offenses, away from sin and to hide me from Thy Face justly irritated against me, hide me in Thy wounds, until Thy anger and just indignation shall have passed away. **Amen.**

TWELFTH **PRAYER**

Our Father - Hail Mary.

O Jesus! Mirror of Truth, symbol of unity, bond of charity, remember the multitude of wounds with which Thou wast afflicted from head to foot, torn and reddened by the spilling of Thy adorable Blood. O great and universal pain, which Thou didst suffer in Thy virginal flesh for love of us! Sweetest Jesus! What is there that Thou couldst have done for us which Thou has not done!

May the fruit of Thy suffering be renewed in my soul by the faithful remembrance of Thy Passion, and may Thy love increase in my heart each day, until I see Thee in eternity: Thou Who art the treasure of every real good and every joy, which I beg Thee to grant me, O Sweetest Jesus, in heaven. **Amen.**

THIRTEENTH **PRAYER**

Our **Father** **–** **Hail** **Mary.**
O Jesus! Strong Lion, Immortal and Invincible King, remember the pain which Thou didst endure when all Thy strength, both moral and physical, was entirely exhausted, Thou didst bow Thy Head, saying: "It is consummated!"

Through this anguish and grief, I beg of Thee Lord Jesus, to have mercy on me at the hour of my death when my mind will be greatly troubled and my soul will be in anguish. **Amen.**

FOURTEENTH **PRAYER**

Our **Father** **–** **Hail** **Mary.**
O Jesus! Only Son of the Father, Splendour and Figure of His Substance, remember the simple and humble

recommendation.

Thou didst make of Thy Soul to Thy Eternal Father, saying: "Father, into Thy Hands I commend My Spirit!" And with Thy Body all torn, and Thy Heart Broken, and the bowels of Thy Mercy open to redeem us, Thou didst Expire.

By this Precious Death, I beg of Thee O King of Saints, comfort me and help me to resist the devil, the flesh and the world, so that being dead to the world I may live for Thee alone.

I beg of Thee at the hour of my death to receive me, a pilgrim and an exile returning to Thee. **Amen.**

FIFTEENTH **PRAYER**

Our Father – Hail Mary.
O Jesus! True and fruitful Vine! Remember the abundant outpouring of Blood which Thou didst so generously shed from Thy Sacred Body as juice from grapes in a wine press.

From Thy Side, pierced with a lance by a soldier, blood and water issued forth until there was not left in Thy Body a single drop, and finally, like a bundle of myrrh lifted to the top of the Cross Thy delicate Flesh was destroyed, the very Substance of Thy Body withered, and the Marrow of Thy Bones dried up.

Through this bitter Passion and through the outpouring of Thy Precious Blood, I beg of Thee, O Sweet Jesus, to receive my soul when I am in my death agony. **Amen.**

CONCLUSION

O Sweet Jesus! Pierce my heart so that my tears of penitence and love will be my bread day and night; may I be converted entirely to Thee, may my heart be Thy perpetual habitation, may my conversation be pleasing to Thee, and may the end of my life be so praiseworthy that I may merit Heaven and there with Thy saints, praise Thee forever. **Amen.**

Milton Keynes UK
Ingram Content Group UK Ltd.
UKHW020744080324
438959UK00014B/582